# A PHOTOGRAPHIC GUIDE TO

# BIRDS

## OF

# NEW ZEALAND

## GEOFF MOON

First published in 2002 by New Holland Publishers (NZ) Ltd
Auckland • Sydney • London • Cape Town

218 Lake Road, Northcote, Auckland, New Zealand
Unit 1, 66 Gibbes Street, Chatswood, NSW 2067, Australia
86–88 Edgware Road, London W2 2EA, United Kingdom
80 McKenzie Street, Cape Town 8001, South Africa

www.newhollandpublishers.co.nz

Copyright © 2002 in text: Geoff Moon
Copyright © 2002 in photography: Geoff Moon
Copyright © 2002 New Holland Publishers (NZ) Ltd

ISBN: 978 1 877246 58 6

Publishing manager: Christine Thomson
Design and typesetting: Julie McDermid
Editor: Brian O'Flaherty

Colour reproduction by Pica Digital Pte Ltd, Singapore
Printed by Times Offset (M) Sdn Bhd, Malaysia, on paper sourced from
sustainable forests.

20 19 18 17 16 15 14 13 12

Front cover photograph: tui (*Prosthemadera novaeseelandiae*).
Back cover photograph: New Zealand pigeon (*Hemiphaga novaeseelandiae*).
Spine photograph: kea (*Nestor notabilis*).
Title page photograph: kingfisher (*Halcyon sancta*).

# Contents

# Introduction

The function of this guidebook is to enable the average nature lover to identify the birds inhabiting mainland New Zealand and its offshore islands. It is not intended as a comprehensive guide for serious birdwatchers, who should consult the *Reed Field Guide to New Zealand Birds*, or *Field Guide to the Birds of New Zealand* (Viking), for more detailed information on behavioural habits of individual birds.

The islands of New Zealand were originally part of the Gondwanaland supercontinent. Approximately 80 million years ago, before Australia was inhabited by mammals or snakes, New Zealand began to separate from the Australian continent. As a result New Zealand was then inhabited only by birds, reptiles and invertebrates. Later two species of bats arrived, being the only native mammals.

Because of this isolation in the world, New Zealand retains several species of unique birds from an ancient lineage. An obvious example is the kiwi, which evolved from the ratites of Gondwanaland.

Most of New Zealand's birds are resident and do not migrate. However, many of the tube-nosed species, the petrels and shearwaters, migrate to the North Pacific Ocean after nesting. Immature gannets spend about four years along the Australian coast before returning to their natal colonies to breed.

The main migrants to New Zealand are thousands of waders which, from their nesting grounds in Siberia and Alaska, spend the summer months feeding on rich marine organisms in tidal estuaries, harbours and mudflats.

Two species of cuckoo arrive each spring from the Solomon Islands and the Bismarck Archipelago. These are the long-tailed cuckoo and the shining cuckoo.

Introduced mammalian predators, such as stoats, rats, possums and feral cats, have been responsible for the extinction of some bird species, with other species becoming severely endangered and now only surviving on some of the predator-free offshore islands. Deer, introduced for sporting purposes, have caused considerable damage to some forests and prevented regeneration of seedlings, with a consequent reduction of the food plants available to many bird species.

By far the greatest damage is a result of the rapid spread of the Australian brush-tailed possum. It was once thought to be a vegetarian, causing considerable damage throughout native forests. However, it has recently been discovered that the animals also prey on bird's eggs and their chicks, even occasionally killing adult birds.

Many of our forest birds feed high in the canopy of trees and are difficult to identify without the use of binoculars. Binoculars or small tripod-mounted scopes are also essential tools to aid identification of small migrant waders. All migrant and resident waders are most easily identified at high tide. At this time the rising tide forces the birds from their feeding grounds to seek roosts on shellbanks and sandspits. A close approach to the massed flocks on their roosts is usually possible by keeping a low profile and moving slowly.

Birdwatching, with an increased understanding of the birds' behaviour, is an endless source of fascination and wonder.

# Classification of New Zealand birds

All animals are grouped into specific sections according to their anatomy. Closely related species are listed as a genus, while related genera are grouped together as a family. These families, in turn, are grouped to form an order.

The first part of a bird's scientific name is its genus, and the second name refers to the species. In some cases a third name is given which refers to a subspecies. As an example, when giving a scientific name to a New Zealand parrot, the kaka, the genus is *Nestor*, the species is *meridionalis*. As there are subspecies for the North Island and South Island kaka, the subspecies name for the North Island kaka is *septentrionalis* and for the South Island subspecies it is *meridionalis*. The closely related kea is grouped in the same genus *Nestor*, with its species name *notabilis*, with no third name, as there are no subspecies of the kea.

Birds in this guidebook are dealt with in taxonomic order, following that listed in the *Checklist of the Birds of New Zealand*, third edition, compiled by the Checklist Committee (E.G. Turbott, Convenor) of the Ornithological Society of New Zealand (published by Random Century). For ease of arrangement, in some instances the order has not been followed strictly.

In a few instances the names of orders have been updated. According to the bird's anatomy, the list begins with the kiwi and finishes with the rook, one of the passerine birds.

## Order STRUTHIONIFORMES

In the family Apterygidae, all species are flightless and lack a keel on the sternum, on which wing muscles are normally attached. New Zealand once had 11 species of moa listed under this order. All moa are now extinct, and one, the giant moa, was the world's largest living bird, considerably larger than the ostrich. Today the kiwi is listed under this order.

## Order PODICIPEDIFORMES

This order includes the entirely aquatic grebes (family Podicipedidae). Their legs are placed well back on the body with the toes being lobe-webbed, with the result that the birds are extremely efficient swimmers and divers. They seldom fly during daytime but migrate to different stretches of water at night.

## Order PROCELLARIIFORMES

This order comprises the pelagic tube-nosed seabirds which have tube-like nostrils placed on the upper bill. Many species in this order inhabit the seas surrounding New Zealand. All species are pelagic, spending their lives roaming the oceans and only come to land during the nesting season. Species in this order range in size from the huge albatrosses (family Diomedeidae) through the smaller petrels and shearwaters (family Procellariidae) to the tiny storm petrels (family Hydrobatidae).

Most birds in this group possess wings with long forearms, especially adapted for gliding flight, although the storm petrels which 'dance' on the water and the small diving petrels have shorter wings.

## Order SPHENISCIFORMES

This order comprises the penguins, which are only found in the southern hemisphere (family Spheniscidae). New Zealand is home to many species of penguins, most found in the outlying subantarctic islands. Included among these is the world's rarest penguin, the yellow-eyed penguin, some of which nest in the South Island. All penguins have wings that are modified as powerful flippers, enabling them to swim rapidly in search of fish.

## Order PELECANIFORMES

Many species in this order inhabit New Zealand. The conspicuous gannet (family Sulidae) are common around these coasts, and three mainland nesting colonies have been formed here. Thirteen species of shag or cormorant (family Phalacrocoracidae) occupy coastal and wetland areas. Many endemic species inhabit outlying islands, and the rarest, the New Zealand king shag, with a total of only 500, is confined to three islands in the Marlborough Sounds.

The feathers of shags are not fully waterproofed. After a session of underwater fishing they need to periodically perch with outspread wings to dry their plumage. Some species, the pink-footed shags, are found only in marine environments while others, like the little shags and little black shags, fish in fresh as well as salt water.

## Order CICONIIFORMES

Six species of heron (family Ardeidae) are found in New Zealand, with the white-faced heron being by far the most common and the white heron occurring in smaller numbers. The small cattle egret migrates to and from Australia, but to date has not bred in New Zealand. The nankeen night heron and the Australasian bittern are classed in a subfamily of this order. The royal spoonbill (family Threskiornithidae) has increased in number during recent years.

All species in this order are characterised by long necks and legs. The spoonbills fly with their necks outstretched, whereas the neck of the herons is folded back during flight.

## Order ANSERIFORMES

Swans, geese and ducks (family Anatidae) are grouped in this order. All members of this family possess fully webbed feet and are strong fliers. The exception is the flightless Auckland Island and Campbell Island teal, the latter being one of the world's rarest ducks, with a total population of fewer than 100 birds.

## Order FALCONIFORMES
The New Zealand falcon (family Falconidae) and the Australasian harrier (family Accipitridae) are the only diurnal birds of prey that exist here. The New Zealand falcon is endemic. Like most falcons, it has longish pointed wings and a rapid flight. Prey is caught by striking it in mid-air. Falcons seldom take carrion, as taken by the slow soaring harrier. The Australasian harrier is common throughout Australasia, southern New Guinea and some Pacific islands.

## Order GALLIFORMES
This order comprises the game birds and these were all introduced to New Zealand. The California quail, chukor, brown quail and ring-necked pheasant all belong to the family Phasianidae. The chukor is found only in the drier, rocky areas of the South Island. All species have short, rounded wings and fly rapidly. All are mainly seed eaters, but occasionally take foliage and insects.

Other birds in this order are the turkey, the peafowl and the guineafowl. A few of these domestic species have become feral in some regions.

## Order GRUIFORMES
Several species of rail belong to the family Rallidae. The flightless endemic takahe was thought to be extinct, but was rediscovered in 1948 in the Murchison Ranges of Fiordland. The endemic weka is also flightless, although it possesses short wings. The banded rail, spotted crake and pukeko are cosmopolitan species. The Australian coot, which introduced itself to New Zealand, and is widespread, is the most aquatic of the rails.

## Order CHARADRIIFORMES
South Island pied oystercatchers are by far the commonest wading bird with an estimated population nearing 100,000 birds. The endemic variable oystercatcher, which exists in different plumage phases, varying from black to pied, is not so common, only inhabiting coastal regions. Both species belong to the family Haematopodidae.

The common pied stilt and the extremely endangered black stilt are in the family Recurvirostridae. The black stilt is the world's rarest wader. The dotterels and plovers, which include the unique endemic wrybill, are grouped in the family Charadriidae.

The family Scolopacidae includes the migrant waders that nest in the northern hemisphere and spend the summer in New Zealand, feeding in marine mudflats, estuaries and harbours. They range in size from the eastern curlew, the largest migrant wader, to the diminutive red-necked stint. The family also includes the many species of sandpiper, the two species of tattler and the most numerous of the visiting waders, the godwits and knots.

This order also includes the skuas, gulls and terns. Skuas belong to the family Stercorariidae, while the gulls and terns belong to the family Laridae. Members of the last mentioned families all have webbed feet.

## Order COLUMBIFORMES
This order includes pigeons and doves. The only endemic species is the New Zealand pigeon. Other species in the order have been introduced to New Zealand. All belong to the family Columbidae.

## Order PSITTACIFORMES
Included in this order are the native parrots and parakeets as well as a few caged birds which have escaped and become established in the wild. The sulphur-crested cockatoo, an Australian bird, is now well established in several North Island locations and the galah, a more recent escapee, is established on the east coast near Auckland. Both birds belong to the family Cacatuidae. All endemic and native parrots and parakeets as well as the introduced rosella parakeet are listed in subfamilies of the family Psittacidae. All species in this order nest in holes in mature trees, some in holes or cavities in the ground.

## Order CUCULIFORMES
New Zealand's two migratory cuckoos belonging to the family Cuculidae are the shining cuckoo and the larger long-tailed cuckoo. These birds lay an egg in individual nests of other small passerine endemic birds, leaving them to foster their chicks. Both species migrate to and from the Solomon Islands, with some long-tailed cuckoos flying on to islands in the Bismarck Archipelago.

## Order STRIGIFORMES
Only two owls inhabit New Zealand, both in the family Strigidae. These are the native morepork, found in the North and South Islands, and the introduced German or little owl, which is confined to the South Island. New Zealand's larger laughing owl is thought to be extinct.

Owls, with the downy edges to their flight feathers, fly silently. This feature, combined with acute hearing and eyesight, make them efficient nocturnal predators.

## Order CORACIIFORMES
New Zealand's common native sacred kingfisher and the larger introduced Australian kookaburra are included in the family Alcedinidae. Kookaburras, which were first introduced to Kawau Island, are only found north of Auckland. The sacred kingfisher is more common in the North Island, where it occupies a range of habitats from marine harbours and open country to wetlands and forests.

## Order PASSERIFORMES

This order embraces the largest number of families and species of birds in the world. They are known as the perching birds, all possessing three toes pointing forwards and one backwards. Many passerines are songbirds, varying in size from the tiny rifleman to the large introduced rook. There are 33 species of passerine birds on mainland New Zealand and offshore islands, with these being grouped into 20 different families.

The family Acanthisittidae includes the New Zealand wrens, the rifleman and rock wren. The bush wrens are now extinct. The last bush wren was seen in 1972 on an island off Stewart Island.

The only member in New Zealand of the family Alaudidae is the introduced skylark, which is common in pastoral areas.

The welcome swallow of the family Hirundinidae introduced itself to New Zealand in 1949 and is now widespread. It was first found breeding here in 1958, under a road bridge in Northland.

The New Zealand pipit, which is sometimes confused with the introduced skylark, belongs to the family Motacillidae. It inhabits rougher pastures, coastal dunes and alpine regions.

Many of the passerine species were introduced to New Zealand, another being the dunnock or hedge sparrow, a bird quite unlike the common house sparrow. The dunnock has a long thin pointed beak and is insectivorous. It belongs to the family Prunellidae.

The family Muscicapidae includes the common blackbird and the song thrush. Both were introduced from Britain in the 1860s.

The secretive fernbird, which inhabits swamplands, belongs to the family Sylviidae. The bird is unusual in that the barbs of its tail feathers are disjointed, giving the tail a fernlike appearance.

Two species of the family Pachycephalidae are the endemic whitehead, found only in the North Island, and the less common yellowhead, which inhabits South Island beech forests. The third member of the family is the common brown creeper, which is found in South Island scrublands and forests.

The endemic grey warbler (family Pardalotidae), one of the smallest birds, is the only New Zealand bird to build an enclosed, hanging nest. It is a foster parent to the egg of the parasitic shining cuckoo.

The familiar New Zealand fantail, of the family Monarchidae, commonly appears with a brownish pied plumage, but in the South Island a black colour form also occurs.

Robins and tomtits belong to the family Petroicidae (formerly Eopsaltriidae). The male tomtit is pied with a white wing bar and females are brownish with a white wing bar. The South Island male has a yellow tinge to its breast. The New Zealand robin is the largest of the insectivorous songbirds. The endangered black robin, which was miraculously saved from extinction, inhabits only two islands of the outlying Chatham Islands.

New Zealand's only member of the family Zosteropidae is the small silvereye. These birds self-introduced from Australia in 1856 and are now very common.

New Zealand's true honeyeaters, the bellbird and tui, belong to the family Meliphagidae. The bellbird is widely distributed in New Zealand. The bird was previously absent from Northland, apart from its offshore islands. Now, due to predator control, bellbirds have introduced themselves to many forested areas of eastern Northland. They are fine songsters. The tui is also a forest bird, although uncommon in beech forests. It frequently visits suburban gardens to take nectar from native and exotic flowers.

The stitchbird was previously included in Meliphagidae but following DNA testing is now classed in the family Notiomystidae, of which it is the sole member. It previously survived only on Little Barrier Island, having been eliminated from the mainland by mammalian predators. Successful transfers have since been made to other predator-free islands and mainland 'islands'.

The family Emberizidae is represented here by the introduced common yellowhammer and the cirl bunting. The latter is found mainly in drier districts of the South Island. This bird occurs more commonly in New Zealand than in Britain, its country of origin.

The true finches, all introduced from Britain, are grouped in the family Fringillidae. The smallest of these is the redpoll, which like the greenfinch and goldfinch frequent the open country. In winter months, very large flocks of goldfinches congregate to feed on the seeds of grasses and thistles. Chaffinches are the only member of the finch family which ventures into forests.

The family Ploceidae is represented by the ubiquitous house sparrow.

The common starling, introduced with other European birds, and the Indian myna belong to the family Sturnidae.

New Zealand's unique wattle birds, which included the extinct huia, belong to the family Callaeidae. Other wattle birds are the North and South Island saddleback and the North Island kokako. The South Island kokako is believed to be extinct, in spite of possible sightings. The kokako inhabits several areas of native forest, but the saddleback survives only on predator-free islands. The kokako is the largest of the native songbirds, with its song being the most melodious of all songsters.

The family Cracticidae is represented by the introduced Australian magpie, which occurs as two subspecies, the white-backed and the black-backed. The two often interbreed. The bird is predatory on ground-nesting birds.

Family Corvidae is represented here by the introduced rook. As the birds increased in number and caused considerable damage to crops, they were declared a pest, with many being exterminated.

## Bird habitats and distribution

Within a relatively small landmass, New Zealand encompasses several different environments in which birds live and breed.

The offshore islands, many of them predator-free, provide homes for some bird species which have been eliminated on the mainland, while the surrounding seas support many species of tube-nosed birds, ranging from albatrosses to tiny storm petrels.

New Zealand has a long, indented coastline of rocky shores, sandy beaches, estuaries and mudflats. All these habitats provide suitable feeding and nesting grounds for gulls, terns and many species of waders, both indigenous and migrant.

Inland, the wetlands that include swamps, lagoons, rivers and lakes support a great variety of waterfowl, waders and other birds.

Large areas of agricultural pastures, arable land and orchards are home to several bird species, particularly introduced passerines.

Extensive tracts of native forest remain, some unmodified, others regenerating after being logged for timber. These forests are inhabited by many endemic forest birds. Also, some of the exotic pine plantation forests are occupied by several native and introduced insectivorous birds.

Much of New Zealand, particularly the South Island, is mountainous. The alpine herbfields provide habitats for a number of endemic, native and introduced birds, while the forests of the foothills are valuable environments for many other birds.

Some species of birds occupy many of these varied habitats. For instance, kingfishers are found on the coast, in wetlands, in agricultural pastures and even in the depths of the forests. Similarly, some wading birds occupy different habitats according to the season, with certain locations favoured for breeding and others as preferred feeding grounds.

# How to use this book

This book illustrates and describes the birds that inhabit, or visit, the three main islands of New Zealand, as well as its offshore islands.

For information on the species inhabiting the subantarctic islands, the Kermadecs and Chatham Islands, the reader should refer to the comprehensive guidebooks listed in the Further Reading at the end of this book.

The approximate size of each bird is given in centimetres, and this is the length from the tip of a bird's bill to the tip of its tail, and includes in some instances the length of its legs, if they extend beyond the tail. These measurements are approximate, because in some of the larger birds there is a difference in size between the sexes.

Generally photographs are not captioned, except to indicate different plumage phases, immature birds rather than adults, distinctive differences between male and female birds, specific ages of chicks, or to otherwise facilitate understanding.

The illustration below shows the main parts of a bird used in descriptions of plumage and anatomy.

*Parts of a bird*

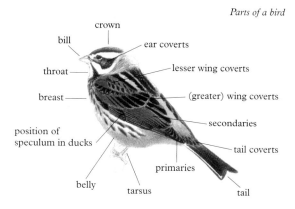

crown

bill

ear coverts

throat

lesser wing coverts

breast

(greater) wing coverts

secondaries

position of speculum in ducks

tail coverts

primaries

belly

tarsus

tail

# Glossary

**Aquatic** Frequenting water.

**Arboreal** Frequenting trees.

**Carrion** Dead animals, e.g. fish on a beach, animal killed by traffic.

**Cere** The fleshy covering of the upper bill of some birds.

**Cosmopolitan** Inhabiting many countries.

**Covey** A small flock of game birds which feed and roost together.

**Crepuscular** Active at dawn and dusk.

**Cryptic** Colouring which merges with the surroundings; camouflage.

**Decurved** Curved downwards.

**Eclipse plumage** Dull plumage acquired after breeding.

**Endangered** Birds likely to become extinct if not carefully managed.

**Endemic** Living and breeding in one country, e.g. kiwi is endemic to New Zealand, emu is endemic to Australia.

**Exotic** Introduced.

**Extinct** No longer in existence.

**Feral** A domestic species living in the wild.

**Flight feathers** The long, well-developed feathers of the wing and tail; the primary and secondary feathers of the wing.

**Immature** A young bird in a plumage stage between juvenile and adult.

**Insectivorous** Feeding on insects and spiders.

**Invertebrates** Animals without a spinal column, e.g. insects, spiders, earthworms, crustaceans.

**Juvenile** Young bird in its first plumage.

**Fledge** Fully feathered and able to fly or run (kiwi).

**Lamellae** Sieve-like appendages on the edge of the bill, used to filter food, e.g. shoveler duck.

**Lek** A place of courtship where males call or perform to attract females for mating, e.g. kakapo and some game birds.

**Migrant** A species which moves to another region to feed after nesting.

**Mollusc** An invertebrate which has a soft body and often a hard outer shell, e.g. snail and some marine shellfish.

**Mustelid** Member of the polecat genus, e.g. stoat, ferret, weasel.

**Omnivorous** Eating a variety of animal and vegetable food.

**Pelagic** Frequenting the open seas.

**Plankton** Small marine organisms, including both animal and vegetable.

**Predator** A mammal or bird which preys on other animals or birds and/or eggs.

**Raptor** A bird of prey.

**Regurgitate** Food that has been partly digested and brought back to the mouth.

**Scrape** A shallow depression in the ground to be used as a nest.

**Speculum** Colourful markings on the secondary feathers of the wing on ducks.

**Subspecies** A geographical population of a species, bearing some slight differences from others of the species.

**Taxonomy** The science of classifying organisms according to their anatomy and natural relationships.

**Threatened** Species that are declining or low in numbers.

**Wattles** Coloured fleshy tissue on either side of the gape of the bill, e.g. kokako, saddleback.

# Kiwi

The kiwi, New Zealand's national symbol, is the most unusual of the ancient flightless ratites (birds without a keel on the breastbone). Kiwi have hairlike body feathers and only vestiges of wings. They are unique in being the only bird in the world with nostrils situated at the tip of a very long bill. With this facility and an acute sense of hearing, the kiwi is able to locate earthworms and grubs several centimetres below the surface of the soil. Its feet, which lack a hind toe, are very strong and enable the bird to run rapidly as well as to exert a forceful kick when attacked by predators. The feet may also be used for digging. Kiwi are remarkable in that they possess two functional ovaries, each producing an egg. Due to predation of kiwi chicks, particularly in Northland, a recovery programme has been established. This entails removing eggs from kiwi nests and incubating them. The kiwi then lay another clutch. When hatched the kiwi chick is hand reared for several months, and is released back into the wild when large enough to protect itself against most predators.

*Brown kiwi.*

*Brown kiwi, four-day-old chick.*

Although the brown kiwi is the most common of the three main species of kiwi, its numbers have recently been markedly reduced with predation by stoats, as well as by feral cats and dogs. The largest populations of brown kiwi are found in Northland and Stewart Island. Brown kiwi are nocturnal in habit, with the exception of the Stewart Island species, which often feed during the day. Their diet consists of earthworms, insects and their larvae and spiders. They also eat ripe fallen fruit. When feeding, the birds breathe with a snuffling sound as they scent for food in the litter of the forest floor. They lay one or two very large eggs per clutch, the second egg often being laid two or three weeks after the first. The nest site is usually in a burrow or the hollow of a fallen tree. Incubation, which varies from 70 to 80 days, is performed by the male bird. However, with the Stewart Island species, incubation is shared by the sexes and sometimes by offspring from a previous clutch.

## Great spotted kiwi *Apteryx haastii* 45–47 cm

This is the largest and least studied of the kiwi. It inhabits the forests of north-west Nelson and the South Island west coast, as far south as Arthur's Pass. As with other kiwi species, the female is the larger of the sexes. It feeds on a variety of insects and their larvae, earthworms and fallen forest fruit. It has also been reported to feed on freshwater crayfish, taken from shallow forest streams. Great spotted kiwi lay only one egg per clutch in a shallow burrow, beneath the roots of trees, or sometimes in hollow fallen logs. The call of the male bird is a high-pitched, loud, ascending whistle, usually producing an immediate response from the female, in a lower-pitched vibrating call.

## Little spotted kiwi *Apteryx owenii* 30 cm

The small size of the little spotted kiwi makes it vulnerable to predation, and it was eliminated from the mainland soon after European settlement, although some survived in the forests of Westland at the turn of the 20th century. The bird was saved from extinction by the introduction of a few birds to Kapiti Island, where numbers now exceed 1000, and many have been transferred to a number of offshore islands. The little spotted kiwi nests in burrows. They lay the largest egg per bodyweight of any bird (23 per cent of its bodyweight). Some clutches contain two eggs, the second being laid about three weeks after the first. The call is a high-pitched, vibrating, ascending whistle.

### Australasian crested grebe *Podiceps cristatus* 50 cm

This subspecies of the cosmopolitan grebes is now found only in the South Island, where it inhabits subalpine lakes east of the Southern Alps. A few birds frequent lowland lakes in Westland. In winter many birds congregate on lowland lakes, such as Lake Forsyth. Crested grebes feed on fish and aquatic invertebrates by diving neatly from the surface, remaining submerged for up to 50 seconds. The birds are usually seen in pairs, and during courtship they display by erecting their neck ruff and head crest, shaking their heads and emitting a moaning cry. The birds nest from late October to January, in a bulky structure composed of sticks, rushes and waterweeds. This is frequently attached to submerged branches of willow. A clutch of up to six eggs is laid in early summer and incubation, lasting around four weeks, is shared by the sexes. The bird covers its eggs with waterweed to camouflage the nest. This results in the eggs becoming stained a brownish colour. As with other grebes, the chicks at intervals are often carried on the back of one of the parents, while the other dives for food. Chicks are often fed small feathers with their fish diet, presumably to coat sharp bones.

PODICIPEDIDAE

Like other grebes, the endemic New Zealand dabchick is entirely aquatic, only coming to land to nest. All grebes are extremely efficient swimmers and divers. Their legs are placed well back on the body and the flattened toes are lobe-webbed. This feature enables them to swim very rapidly when they feed submerged, on a diet of small fish, tadpoles, aquatic invertebrates and molluscs. New Zealand dabchicks are now found only in the North Island, with large numbers inhabiting the west coast dune lakes, the lakes of the Rotorua district and Lake Taupo. After their protracted breeding season from early July to March, birds often flock together. When migrating to other lakes, they fly only at night. Recently, dabchicks have crossed metropolitan areas to inhabit urban lakes, such as Western Springs. Here they are breeding successfully. Nests are composed of rushes and waterweeds, anchored to reeds. Some nests are built under boat sheds or marina wharfs. Two or three eggs form the usual clutch, which is incubated for just over three weeks by both parents in turn. As with all grebes, when the nest is vacated, the eggs are covered and eggs soon become stained. Chicks are carried on the back of one parent while the other dives for food. However, chicks learn to dive at an early age.

**Australian little grebe** *Tachybaptus novaehollandiae* 25 cm

This small grebe introduced itself to New Zealand 30 years ago. It is now established on several lakes and small raupo-fringed ponds in Northland. A few birds were noted on some South Island lakes, but did not become settled. This grebe is far more wary than the slightly larger New Zealand dabchick. When seen on the same stretch of water, the Australian grebe quickly disappears into the surrounding rushes or sometimes dives, keeping only its head above the surface. The bird is easily distinguished from the New Zealand dabchick by a prominent 'teardrop' yellow patch of skin between the eye and base of its bill. The bird's diet consists of small fish and aquatic invertebrates. Like the large crested grebe, the Australian little grebe sometimes feeds small feathers to its chicks. It nests from December to March, constructing a floating nest of weeds, often anchored to rushes. Both birds share incubation of the two- or three-egg clutch, which hatches after 23 days. Chicks are able to swim soon after hatching and are often carried on one parent's back while the other dives for food.

The **hoary-headed grebe**, *Poliocephalus poliocephalus*, a bird of similar size and habits to the New Zealand dabchick, is an Australian species that has occurred sporadically in New Zealand since the 1970s. It has nested in the South Island on occasions, but has not become established. The bird can be recognised by its slim appearance, and during the breeding season, by the silver streaky feathers on its head.

## Northern royal albatross *Diomedea sanfordi* 115 cm

The albatrosses are the largest flying birds, and with the smaller albatrosses or mollymawks are the largest of the pelagic tubenosed seabirds. They are common in the seas around the subantarctic islands and the Chathams, where many species nest. About 25 pairs of the northern royal albatross nest at Taiaroa Head on the Otago Peninsula, the only nesting site on an inhabited mainland. Birds start breeding when eight or nine years old. A single white egg is laid at the end of October or early November. Each of the pair takes turns to incubate for periods of two to 10 days, until the chick hatches after about 80 days of incubation. As the chick, which is fed on regurgitated squid and fish, does not fledge until it is about eight months old, the adults only breed every second year. After fledging, birds move eastward towards South America and the southern oceans. Some immature birds return to their natal nesting sites when three or four years old. They often perform mock courtship displays, but do not breed until they are at least eight years old.

## Shy mollymawk (White-capped mollymawk)
*Thalassarche cauta* 90 cm

This small albatross is common around the waters of Stewart Island where it follows fishing boats close inshore. It also frequents coastal waters further north. There are four species of the shy mollymawk and three of them nest in colonies, mainly on subantarctic islands, and on an islet off the Chathams coast. Like other mollymawks it feeds mainly on squid, krill and fish. It is attracted to fishing trawlers where it feeds on fish or fish waste thrown overboard. They start breeding in early summer, laying one egg on a mound of seaweed, mud and guano. Both sexes share incubation which lasts for about 10 weeks, and the chick fledges when four and a half months old.

## Buller's mollymawk *Thalassarche bulleri* 80 cm

An endemic species, this is slightly smaller than the shy mollymawk. These birds are often seen together around fishing boats off Stewart Island, but the Buller's is easily distinguished by distinctive golden-yellow margins to its bill. There are two subspecies: the northern Buller's mollymawk has a silver-grey colouring to its forehead, compared with the whiter forehead of the southern subspecies. The northern Buller's mollymawk nests on the Three Kings Islands in the north of New Zealand as well as the Chathams, while the southern subspecies nests on some of the southern islands. Nesting is similar to that of the shy mollymawk, but the chick usually fledges when about five months of age. The bird's diet consists of squid, fish and krill.

21

**Northern giant petrel** *Macronectes halli* 90 cm

The northern giant petrel is the largest of the petrels, approaching the size of the mollymawks. But with its bulkier body and shorter wings, it lacks the graceful, soaring flight of the albatrosses. The giant petrel has a massive bill with long tube nostrils extending along the upper surface. It is the only petrel to feed on land, scavenging dead seals and carrion. The aggressive males also kill and eat penguin chicks and take eggs from nesting birds. Females have slightly different feeding habits, taking fish and squid. Unlike the smaller petrels, giant petrels do not use burrows for nesting. The northern giant petrel nests in loose colonies, mainly on Campbell Island, building a cup-shaped nest of seaweed and tussock grasses. It lays a single white egg in early October or November which is incubated by both sexes in turn for nine weeks. The chick is brooded for the first two weeks only, and fledges in late summer when four months old.

**Flesh-footed shearwater** *Puffinus carneipes* 45 cm

This dark brown shearwater is the one most likely to be seen in North Island waters during summer months. The birds are usually seen singly, as they glide effortlessly with their wing tips just clear of the water. Recreational fishers, fishing from boats, often see them diving after their baited lines. In winter months most flesh-footed shearwaters migrate to the north or western Pacific Ocean. They return in October or November, to nest on several islands off the North Island east coast, with the largest number nesting on the islands of the Hen and Chickens group. They also nest on several subtropical islands in the southern Pacific and Indian Oceans. One white egg is laid in a burrow dug in soft soil, and is incubated by both sexes for about seven weeks. The chick is fed on a regurgitated paste of fish and then fledges when it is about three months old.

**Buller's shearwater** *Puffinus bulleri* 46 cm

An endemic species, Buller's shearwater is common in northern east coast waters during summer months. They can be recognised by a distinctive brown 'W' pattern across the top surface of the grey wings. They are seen singly or in small flocks. The population of Buller's shearwaters is estimated to exceed 2.5 million birds, yet their only known nesting site is on the Poor Knights Islands, off the east coast of Northland. Like other petrels and shearwaters they come ashore to nest only after dark and lay a single white egg in a burrow, in November. Parents take turns to incubate, for spells of four or five days. The chick hatches after seven weeks and fledges when over three months old. Food consists of small fish, krill and jellyfish. Buller's shearwater does not dive, but feeds just below the surface of the sea. After nesting, in late April most birds migrate to the northern Pacific Ocean, spending up to four months feeding in the waters of the west coasts of North America. Some are seen off the coast of Chile.

## Sooty shearwater *Puffinus griseus* 44 cm

The sooty shearwater is one of the world's most common birds, with a population estimated to exceed 20 million. It breeds in many locations in the south Pacific and Atlantic oceans. In the southern winter the birds migrate to feed in the north Pacific and a few migrate to the north Atlantic. It feeds on krill, squid and small fish, which they capture by diving from the surface of the water to depths of a few metres. Several million sooty shearwaters breed in New Zealand, most on islands around Stewart Island and subantarctic islands. Their nesting and feeding habits are similar to those of other shearwaters, coming ashore to their nesting burrows after dark. They begin cleaning their nesting burrows in soft soil and lay one white egg in November. Both sexes share incubation for periods of two to four days. The chick hatches after seven and a half weeks and is fed on regurgitated fish paste. The chicks are a traditional food for Maori, and large numbers of 'mutton-birds' are harvested from colonies in the southern islands, without any apparent impact on the population. During their migration north after nesting, rafts of sooty shearwaters, stretching for several kilometres, can be seen from east coast locations.

### Fluttering shearwater *Puffinus gavia* 33 cm

Fluttering shearwater is endemic, breeding only in New Zealand. It is common in northern waters, in Cook Strait and the Marlborough Sounds. In winter it is often seen as far south as Stewart Island. After the nesting season many birds migrate northwards to the Australian coast. Nesting begins in early September on many predator-free islands off the east coast of northern New Zealand. As with other shearwaters, one egg is laid in a burrow and incubated by each parent in turn. Another endemic shearwater, which is difficult to distinguish from the fluttering shearwater, is the less common **Hutton's shearwater,** *Puffinus huttoni*. This bird, only discovered in 1965, nests in burrows high in the Seaward Kaikoura Ranges. It lays one egg in late October, although nesting is sometimes delayed due to late snowfalls.

### Little shearwater *Puffinus assimilis* 30 cm

The smallest of the native shearwaters, little shearwater's colouring somewhat resembles that of the fluttering shearwater, but it is the only shearwater with pale blue legs and feet. New Zealand populations more commonly inhabit northern coastal waters. A North Island subspecies is common in the Hauraki Gulf and Bay of Plenty, nesting on several offshore islands. The little shearwater nests only on predator-free islands. It is a winter nester, the single egg being laid in a burrow in June or July in northern regions and in September in the south.

## Cape pigeon *Daption capense* 40 cm

Cape pigeon is a very distinctive member of the tube-nosed seabirds and, with its black and white chequered plumage and white underparts, is easily identified. It mainly inhabits the southern seas, but is seen in coastal water of the north during winter months. The cape pigeon feeds on krill, small fish and sometimes squid as well as offal from fishing boats. It has derived this name because of its rapid pigeon-like pecking of food, when sitting

on the water's surface. Unlike shearwaters, cape pigeons nest on cliff ledges or in rock crevices, laying one white egg that is incubated for about six and a half weeks by each parent in turn. The chick fledges when it is about seven weeks old.

## Broad-billed prion *Pachyptila vittata* 28 cm

The prions are small blue-grey petrels with a distinctive 'W' marking on the upper wings, a feature noticeable only at close quarters. Prions are usually seen in dense flocks in coastal waters. The broad-billed prion feeds by skimming over the water surface, swinging its head from side to side while immersing its broad bill to scoop plankton. This is filtered by lamellae at the edges of the bird's bill. The broad-billed prion nests in burrows on islands around Stewart Island, and vast numbers nest in the Chathams. One egg is laid in August or September.

**Black petrel** *Procellaria parkinsoni* 46 cm

The endemic black petrel ranges far out to sea, and is seen·in inland waters only during the nesting season, when a single egg is laid in a burrow in December. The main population nests on Great Barrier Island in the outer Hauraki Gulf. Others nest high on Little Barrier Island. The rare endemic **Westland black petrel**, ***Procellaria westlandica***, is the largest of the petrels which nest in burrows. The only known nesting site is in the hills south of the Punakaiki River in Westland. Unlike the black petrel, it nests in winter, laying a single egg in May or June. Both species, when seen at sea, are somewhat similar to the commoner flesh-footed shearwater, but can be distinguished by their stronger flight and a black-tipped bill.

**Grey-faced petrel** *Pterodroma macroptera* 41 cm

There are two subspecies of this large petrel, with one being the most common petrel, especially in northern New Zealand waters. Squid, caught at night, forms the main diet but small fish are also taken. When disturbed from resting on the water, the bird rises effortlessly and soars in wide arcs. The grey-faced petrel is one of the few tube-nosed seabirds which still nests on the mainland. In the North Island several colonies nest in burrows on forested and scrub-covered headlands, some close to populated areas. They are winter nesters, laying a single egg in a burrow in July. Large colonies also nest on the northern offshore islands. After nesting, grey-faced petrels remain in southern waters.

## Cook's petrel *Pterodroma cookii* 29 cm

The endemic Cook's petrel is one of the 27 species of gadfly petrels that mainly inhabit the southern oceans. All have short, heavily hooked bills and a distinctive, batlike flight. Between rapid wingbeats, they hold their wings stiffly, gliding in wide arcs. Cook's petrel is usually seen in waters to the east of New Zealand, migrating to the northern and eastern Pacific each autumn after nesting. The largest nesting colonies are sited on Little Barrier Island where they nest in burrows, laying a single egg in November. A few pairs nest on Great Barrier Island, and the other only known nesting site is to the far south, on Codfish Island. Their diet consists of small fish and squid taken at night when they come to the surface.

## Pycroft's petrel *Pterodroma pycrofti* 28 cm

This petrel is very similar to the Cook's petrel, but is slightly smaller and darker in colour, although they are difficult to differentiate in flight. Pycroft's petrels are an endangered species and breed only on predator-free islands, mainly those off the east coast of Northland and the Mercury Islands. Their feeding and nesting behaviour is similar to that of the Cook's petrel. Pycroft's petrel can be seen in waters off the north-eastern North Island in summer. After nesting they migrate to the north Pacific.

**White-faced storm petrel** *Pelagodroma marina* 20 cm

Storm petrels are the smallest of the tube-nosed seabirds, being smaller than a blackbird. Twenty species inhabit the world's oceans, but the most commonly seen in New Zealand waters is the white-faced storm petrel. It is easily recognised by its method of feeding. The bird dances along just above the water's surface between short glides, with legs held dangling. When feeding against a strong wind it often walks on the water, seizing plankton and small crustaceans. Large numbers nest in burrows on many offshore islands and islets. An estimated one million pairs breed on islands in the Chathams. A single white egg is laid in October or November, which is incubated by both sexes for spells of four or five days. The chick hatches after seven weeks' incubation and fledges when eight weeks old. After nesting, most birds migrate to the tropical waters of the eastern Pacific Ocean. On some islands nesting colonies have been reduced in size due to predation of chicks and adults by rats and native weka. However, colonies on predator-free offshore islands are thriving.

## Yellow-eyed penguin *Megadyptes antipodes* 70 cm

The endemic yellow-eyed penguin is one of the world's rarest penguins. Like other penguins, it is flightless, the wings being modified into powerful flippers which propel the body at speed when fishing under water. The bird walks upright on land, with a wobbling gait. It inhabits the east coast of the South Island, south of Bank's Peninsula, where some pairs nest. It is more common around Stewart Island and the subantarctic islands. Unlike many penguin species which nest in colonies, yellow-eyed penguins nest in isolation. Nests are usually made in clumps of coastal flax or other vegetation, and are vulnerable to predation by stoats and feral cats. One or two pale blue eggs are laid in September or October. Both sexes incubate for about six weeks, with the chicks fledging at nearly 16 weeks, when they are able to swim and fend for themselves. After nesting, the adults indulge in a short period of intensive feeding before coming ashore to hide themselves for about three weeks as they moult their feathers entirely. These fall off in tufts as new plumage develops. During this period the birds remain hidden and do not feed. Another rare endemic, the **Fiordland crested penguin**, *Eudyptes pachyrhynchus*, breeds in a few forested localities on the coast of South Westland and Fiordland.

31

**Blue penguin** *Eudyptula minor* 40 cm

The smallest species of penguin, blue penguin is common around New Zealand coasts. It is often seen resting on the water, sometimes lying on its side and revealing its white underparts. Around the Canterbury coast, the same species of blue penguin show a colour morph, with white edges to their flippers. The blue penguin is the only species of penguin which comes ashore after dark, to either its nest or to moult. Blue penguins swim very rapidly under water in pursuit of small fish and crustaceans. They have been recorded by divers at depths over 50 metres, but they usually fish close to the surface. Most birds nest on offshore islands, particularly in northern New Zealand. On a few offshore islands, some birds choose to nest as far as 500 metres inland, having to make this long journey to their nests each night. However, there are many nesting sites on the mainland, some close to cities, as in Wellington. Unfortunately many nesting birds on the mainland are predated, especially by roaming dogs. Blue penguins nest in shallow burrows, beneath the roots of large trees, in rock crevices and caves, and sometimes under seaside dwellings where their nocturnal noises make this presence unwelcome. In northern areas, penguins often begin nesting in winter months, laying two eggs that are incubated by both sexes for about five weeks. Chicks fledge when about seven or eight weeks old.

**Australasian gannet** *Morus serrator* 90 cm

*Australasian gannet rookery.*

There are three subspecies of gannet that breed in the northern and southern hemispheres, each showing slight differences in plumage colour. The Australasian gannet is common around New Zealand coastal waters, where it can be seen making its spectacular dives for fish and then resting on the surface, often in large flocks. Several nesting colonies are sited on islands around the coast, with the largest on volcanic White Island and on Gannet Island off the North Island west coast. The gannet population is increasing each year, with three thriving mainland colonies: the long established Cape Kidnappers colony in Hawke's Bay, a smaller colony at Farewell Spit, and an easily viewed colony at Muriwai, on Auckland's west coast. Gannets begin congregating at their nesting sites in winter, laying a single egg from September to December. Both sexes take turns at incubating the egg under the web of their feet. Nests are a small mound of seaweed, vegetation and guano. Eggs hatch after six weeks and the chicks fledge when 16 weeks of age, showing at this stage a speckled brown plumage. They instinctively learn to dive for fish as they cross the Tasman Sea to spend four or five years around the coast of Australia. The birds return to breed in their natal colonies when five to six years of age.

## Black shag (Black cormorant) *Phalacrocorax carbo* 88 cm

There are more than 30 species of shags or cormorants world-wide, and 12 species breed in New Zealand. The black shag is a cosmopolitan species, with the New Zealand subspecies commonly seen in coastal regions and on inland lakes. It dives from the surface to feed on a wide variety of fish and crustaceans, usually remaining submerged for 30 to 40 seconds. It nests in colonies, in large nests of sticks in trees overhanging water, or on the ground on small islands in lagoons, or on the cliff ledges of inland lakes. The nesting season extends over several months, with most eggs laid between June and November. The three or four eggs hatch after four weeks' incubation; the chicks are then fed by regurgitation and fledge at seven weeks.

## King shag *Leucocarbo carunculatus* 75 cm

The endemic king shag is one of the rarest shags in the world. It inhabits a few small islets in the deep waters at the head of the Marlborough Sounds. The bird feeds on deep underwater fish such as flounder, sole and blue cod, by diving from the surface and remaining submerged for up to 50 seconds. The nesting season varies from year to year, but occurs usually between May and June. Nests composed of sticks and seaweed glued with guano are built on flat rock platforms. The clutch consists of two or three pale blue eggs, but incubation periods are not known.

## Little black shag *Phalacrocorax sulcirostris* 60 cm

The little black shag is common in the North Island, with few seen in the South Island. They are usually seen in groups, frequenting freshwater lakes, especially in the Rotorua district. They also inhabit sheltered marine regions, particularly when fishing in packs. Several birds herd a shoal of fish and while some dive, those which have just surfaced leapfrog to the front of the advancing pack to dive again. Birds are distinguished from the large black shag by their smaller size, glossy black plumage, long tail and a longer thin bill. The last feature is also a variation from the similarly sized, black plumaged immature little shag. The main food items are fish, especially eels, crustaceans and aquatic insects. When floating on the water, all shags sit very low. This is due to the fact that their feathers are only partially waterproofed, and with a lack of duck-like buoyancy they spend less energy than ducks when fishing submerged. After periods of fishing, all shags perch to dry their plumage, with wings outspread. Little black shags begin nesting in late spring, but nesting in autumn is not uncommon. They often nest in colonies with little shags, building a nest of sticks in trees or bushes close to fresh water. Both sexes take turns in incubating the clutch of three to four eggs.

**Little shag** *Phalacrocorax melanoleucos* 56 cm

*Little shag, pied phase.*

The little shag occurs in several plumage forms. Some are black with a white throat, others in the pied phase show a completely white breast, while some are smudgy with a white throat and distinctively white flecked breast, with often a small head crest evident. The plumage of juvenile little shags is black, but they can be distinguished from the little black shag as their bill is shorter and their black plumage lacks lustre. Unlike little black shags, little shags do not fish in packs. They prefer freshwater habitats and often fish in small ponds and narrow farm ditches where eels are present. They also frequent marine harbours, estuaries and sheltered coastal waters. Little shags nest in large colonies, building a nest of sticks in trees, particularly willows. Some nest in coastal pohutukawa trees along with large pied shags. Others nest inland with little black shags. The nesting season is long. Early nesting begins in July in northern districts, extending to January. A few birds nest in March. The usual clutch of three or four pale blue eggs is incubated by both sexes. Chicks are fed regurgitated fish.

## Stewart Island shag *Leucocarbo chalconotus* 68 cm

*Stewart Island shag, colony.*

The endemic Stewart Island shag inhabits coastal areas on the east of the South Island from North Otago to Stewart Island. Two plumage forms occur, some bronze with a greenish sheen to the feathers, and the other is a pied form, more common in the south. Both colour forms interbreed with a result that resembles the king shag. Stewart Island shags, like king shags, feed mainly on deep-sea dwelling fish, such as flounder and sole. They also take crabs and other crustaceans. Like the spotted shag, they often fish far out at sea, making deep dives where they may be submerged for up to a minute and a half. They nest in colonies, building a nest of seaweed and small sticks cemented with guano. Most colonies are sited on rocky islets and rock platforms. An easily viewed colony is on a rock platform on the north side of the Otago Peninsula, below the royal albatross colony. The clutch of two to three pale blue eggs is usually laid between September and November. Both sexes take turns at incubation, but the incubation period and age at which the chicks fledge have not been recorded.

37

**Spotted shag** *Stictocarbo punctatus* 73 cm

*Spotted shag, nesting colony.*

The strikingly plumaged endemic spotted shag was once uncommom in the North Island, as they were thought to deplete fish stocks and were shot by fishermen. However, following strict protection, the birds are now quite common. Spotted shags are a strictly marine species and are not found inland. They inhabit exposed rocky shores and often feed far out at sea where they capture fish and small squid. The birds dive from the surface, remaining submerged for about 20 seconds, but when feeding in deep water, this period is often up to a minute. The nesting season varies considerably in different regions. In the north, nesting usually begins in early May, with the birds at this time displaying an impressive double-curled head crest. In the South Island, nesting on the volcanic cliff ledges of Banks Peninsula usually begins in September. Some nesting sites, such as one on the cliffs at Bethells Beach on the Auckland west coast, are exposed to winds off the Tasman Sea. Nests are built on cliff ledges or in caves and are composed of sticks and seaweed. Guano is not used as cement. The usual clutch consists of two or three pale blue eggs, incubated for four and a half weeks. Chicks are fed by regurgitation and fledge when about nine weeks old.

**Pied shag** *Phalacrocorax varius* 81 cm

The common pied shag favours sheltered coastal waters and is rarely seen inland, although it inhabits some freshwater lakes not far from the coast. They are more frequently seen in the North Island, although some inhabit the Marlborough Sounds and Banks Peninsula. Pied shags are the least wary of the shags and can often be approached closely when perched on rocks, posts or coastal trees. Their diet consists of a variety of fish, especially eels caught in freshwater lakes. They sometimes fish in shallow water, capturing large flounder which they have difficulty in swallowing whole. They usually fish alone, staying submerged for about 20 seconds. Pied shags have a very extended breeding season and, particularly in the north, nesting may take place during many months of the year. The northern nesting season usually occurs from July to November, with another peak nesting time in autumn. Large colonies nest in sheltered coastal trees, such as pohutukawa in the North Island, with nests in the south often built in pines near the coast. Other nesting sites may be found in willows bordering freshwater lakes. The nesting sites are often shared with a smaller species such as little black and little shags. Three or four turquoise-coloured eggs form the usual clutch. Both sexes incubate for approximately four weeks. Like other shags, the chicks are fed on regurgitated fish, the chick inserting its head deep into the parent's throat. Chicks fledge when about eight weeks old, with parents continuing to feed them for several weeks after they have left the nest.

39

**White-faced heron** *Ardea novaehollandiae* 66 cm

A few white-faced herons, an Australian species, were recorded in New Zealand in the early 1900s and nested in the South Island in the 1940s. However, a large number of birds were self-introduced to northern areas of New Zealand in the late 1940s. They bred successfully and spread widely, including to the outlying Chatham Islands. White-faced herons are now by far the commonest of the heron species. Part of the success of their establishment is the fact that they are able to feed in a variety of habitats, including coastal estuaries, harbours, wetlands and open pastures. They are now often seen feeding in urban parks and school playing fields. White-faced herons feed on a wide-ranging diet, consisting of small fishes, frogs, crustaceans, earthworms and insects. They have a habit, when feeding in shallow tidal pools, of raking with a foot to disturb marine invertebrates. Like other herons, they are equipped with patches of powder down, which are actually disintegrating feathers on their flanks. The birds use this powder to remove fish slime from their bill after catching eels. White-faced herons are early nesters. In northern districts nests are built in June or July and in October or November in the south. Nests consist of large and small sticks built high in pines, macrocarpa trees and tall manuka. Some birds nest in coastal pohutukawa trees. Two to four pale turquoise eggs are incubated for 26 days by both sexes, and chicks fledge when about six weeks of age.

## White heron *Egretta alba* 90 cm

This large heron is a cosmopolitan species inhabiting tropical and temperate regions of the world. The New Zealand population is small, with only one breeding location, in trees on the banks of the Waitangiroto River in Westland. This area of the South Island has a temperate microclimate. After the summer nesting season, birds disperse throughout the country to feed in freshwater streams and lagoons, and on sheltered estuaries as well as mangrove-fringed mudflats. Diet consists of fish, frogs and invertebrates. It has also been reported that they occasionally catch mice and small birds. When seen outside the breeding season, the birds' bills are yellow, as are immature birds. But as the nesting season approaches in September, breeding birds develop back plumes and the bills turn black. Nests are built of sticks and placed in the canopy of trees on the river bank. Some nests are built in the crowns of treeferns. Two to four pale turquoise eggs are laid from late September to November, with both sexes sharing incubation which takes 25 to 26 days. Chicks grip the parent's bill crosswise to receive regurgitated fish. When chicks are small the parent waits to partially digest the food before feeding. Chicks fledge when six and a half weeks old, but stay around to be fed before leaving the colony.

**Reef heron** *Egretta sacra* 66 cm

Reef herons are another cosmopolitan species, inhabiting tropical and temperate regions. They are reasonably common around coastal New Zealand, especially on rocky coastlines, but are only very rarely seen inland. However, their numbers have declined in some parts of the North Island, particularly in the Hauraki Gulf and Manukau Harbour. This is probably due to the disturbance of nesting sites caused by recreational boating, which has increased remarkably in recent years. The birds catch a variety of small fish, especially small flounder and crustaceans. When fishing, they stalk along the tideline jabbing rapidly to catch their prey. At other times they stand motionless in shallow water with their wings outspread, presumably to reduce reflections. They are sometimes seen fishing with white-faced herons, when their stocky body, shorter legs and heavier bill distinguish the two species. Reef herons build a nest of sticks in caves, rock crevices, in clumps of coastal flax or beneath exposed roots of pohutukawa trees. Some cave nests are used year after year and may be over 30 cm in depth. Two or three pale turquoise eggs are laid from September to December, and sometimes in early August in northern coastal areas. Sexes take turns incubating for four weeks, and chicks are fed on regurgitated fish. When about three weeks old chicks wander away from the nest. They fledge when about five weeks old, staying with the parents for several more weeks.

**Nankeen night heron** *Nycticorax caledonicus* 56 cm

This small, stockily built heron is a cosmopolitan species. It is quite common in Australia, from where the small New Zealand population migrated. The nankeen night heron is unusual among herons in that it feeds mainly at night and sometimes in the evening. It favours sheltered marine habitats, especially those bordered by mangroves in the north, and in estuaries and some wetlands further south. Food consists of fish, frogs and insects. During the day they roost in dense-foliaged trees, such as macrocarpa growing close to water. Little is known of their breeding habits in New Zealand, but in recent years several pairs have nested in a small colony in a tributary of the Whanganui River. They build nests composed of sticks, in trees close to the water.

**Little egret** *Egretta garzetta* 60 cm

This small heron, a cosmopolitan species, visits New Zealand in autumn, presumably after nesting in Australia. They leave here in the spring, although some birds have been recorded as staying throughout the summer. Little egrets are usually seen singly, or in very small groups. Their favourite habitat is in sheltered estuaries, but they are also seen at freshwater lagoons. Their feeding methods are attractive to observe. Standing in shallow water, they suddenly begin a routine of quickly dancing and high-stepping with raised wings as they capture small fish, crustaceans and insects. Their flight resembles that of the small cattle egret, flying rapidly, showing their rounded wings and neck retracted. There are no records of little egrets breeding in New Zealand.

43

## **Cattle egret** *Bubulcus ibis* 51 cm

This small heron is very common in many countries throughout the world. Early in the 20th century, the African subspecies spread to the Americas, where they are increasing in North and South America. The subspecies seen in New Zealand and Australia are thought to have spread from Asia. Cattle egrets are found in areas from Northland to Stewart Island, with the largest flocks seen in the Waikato and the Manawatu. Each May, numbers migrate to New Zealand from Australia to spend the winter and spring feeding in flocks among cattle. The birds are usually seen in large flocks, sometimes of more than a hundred. They feed on insects and earthworms disturbed by the feet of grazing cattle. After a spell of feeding the birds rest by perching on fences or in trees. In spring cattle egrets assume a bright buff-coloured nuptial plumage on their crown and neck. In late October or November they return to Australia to nest. There has been no record of nesting in New Zealand.

## Australasian bittern *Botaurus poiciloptilus* 71 cm

Australasian bitterns inhabit swamps and some coastal lagoons. Their numbers have been markedly reduced by the draining of swamplands to produce pastureland. When feeding, their cryptic plumage blends with their habitat of rushes, and when disturbed, they stand with upward-pointing bill, so that they are difficult to distinguish from their surroundings. Bitterns feed on fish, particularly eels, frogs and aquatic invertebrates. The bittern is closely related to the herons. However, their breeding habits are entirely different, with the male taking no part in the incubation or care of the chicks. In spring, the male calls females with a booming sound, repeated at intervals. The female builds a substantial nest composed of rushes and vegetation. Nests are always well concealed, usually in thick beds of raupo or sometimes in coastal beds of sedges. Three to six olive-brown eggs are laid at two-day intervals. Incubation, which takes three and a half weeks, commences with the laying of the second egg so that chicks hatch at intervals and are disproportionate in size. When chicks are small, the parent regurgitates the last (undigested) fish it has caught, and feeds the chicks on the partially digested first-caught fish. She then swallows the undigested fish. Chicks begin to wander from the nest when about two weeks old and finally fledge at about five weeks.

**Royal spoonbill** *Platalea regia* 78 cm

Although spoonbills may resemble herons in some respects, they are not closely related. They are classed in a different family and grouped with ibises. In flight, their necks are fully extended, and not folded backwards as with herons. Until 1975 only a few spoonbills inhabited New Zealand, some nesting in trees near the white heron colony at Okarito. Since that time the population has increased remarkably, following successful breeding in both North and South Islands. The first sizeable nesting colony was located at the Wairau Lagoons in Marlborough. Spoonbills feed by wading in shallow water and swinging their spatulate bills from side to side, filtering small invertebrates and fish. They sometimes capture larger fish with a direct strike. When feeding in fresh water they also capture frogs. Royal spoonbills nest in loose colonies on small, low islands within tidal lagoons, where their nests are occasionally inundated by high tides. Other nesting sites are in low, coastal trees, often near shag colonies. Nests are bulky structures composed of sticks and lined with soft grasses. Two or three white eggs, speckled with brown spots, are laid from October to December. Both sexes incubate for three and a half weeks. Unlike herons, which grip the parent's bill crosswise to receive food, spoonbill chicks insert their short bills into the parent's open bill to receive regurgitated food. Chicks fledge and are able to fly when they are seven weeks old.

**Mute swan** *Cygnus olor* 150 cm

Mute swans were introduced to New Zealand from Europe in the 1860s. Their main population is on Lake Ellesmere, but some birds inhabit small lakes in urban parks and ornamental ponds. Although given the name 'mute', the birds are often quite vocal, sounding a loud 'honk'. Males are sometimes aggressive, 'hissing' to effect. Usually the birds are seen in pairs, but congregate in groups when moulting. With a mainly vegetarian diet, they eat water plants and willow leaves as well as grazing grass and vegetation on lake shores. They are also reported feeding on invertebrates and frogs. Mute swans build enormous nests composed of raupo and other vegetation, sometimes lined with a few feathers. The clutch of six to 10 white eggs is incubated by the female for five weeks and cygnets are able to swim soon after hatching.

**Cape Barren goose** *Cereopsis novaehollandiae* 85 cm

Cape Barren geese were first introduced to New Zealand in 1914, but they did not thrive. They are uncommon, and the few sightings are of birds that have immigrated from Australia. They inhabit open-country wetlands, grazing on pasture grasses. They also take water plants, but spend most of their time on land. Nests are composed of rushes and grasses, and the usual clutch of four to six eggs is incubated by the female. There are no records of birds nesting in the wild, with the main nesting in New Zealand being in semi-captivity.

Black swans were first introduced to New Zealand from Australia in the 1860s, with other birds thought to have migrated from Australia. The birds have thrived and are now seen in their thousands on lakes, lagoons and wetlands throughout the country. They also live in marine habitats, with very large numbers seen on the Vernon Lagoons in Marlborough, on the northern Kaipara Harbour and in tidal waters to the east of Farewell Spit. The swans also inhabit the Chatham Islands. In autumn months, when they moult, the birds congregate for safety on secluded lakes and harbours. Black swans feed on water plants and sometimes graze waterside pasture. In shallow marine habitats they graze eel grass, also feeding on invertebrates. They have a very extended nesting season, with a peak from July to September, but in northern districts nesting often continues sporadically until autumn. Most nest sites are in vegetation close to water, although some nest sites near lakes are on dry land, as far as several metres from the water. The large nest is composed of raupo and coarse grasses, lined with a few feathers. Both sexes share incubation of the clutch of four to 10 pale green eggs. Incubation averages five weeks, with the young cygnets able to swim and leave the nest on the second day after hatching. They remain in a group, closely guarded, especially by the cob. Young birds begin breeding when about two years old.

## Canada goose *Branta canadensis* 100 cm

Canada geese were introduced in the early 20th century for sporting purposes and, like the black swan, have thrived. In parts of the South Island Canada geese have become a pest in agricultural areas, fouling pastures and damaging certain crops. In the duck shooting season, a few thousand birds are shot each year. Recent introductions of Canada geese to Hawke's Bay and the Waikato have resulted in successful breeding, with the bird now spreading to many areas, including a few to Northland. They are often seen flying in 'V' formation and uttering a double honking call. In winter Canada geese flock together in large numbers, and at this time are wary when approached and quickly take flight. Nesting in the South Island takes place from September to November. Most of these nest sites are near the headwaters of the many rivers that flow from the east of the Southern Alps, as well as in the foothills of south Westland. In the North Island nesting sites are usually near wetlands. The nest is built of rushes and coarse grasses and lined with down. Four to eight white eggs form the usual clutch, incubated by the female for just over four weeks. After hatching, the goslings remain with the parents for a few days and later join large crèches, which adults take turns at guarding.

**Paradise shelduck** *Tadorna variegata* 63 cm

*Paradise shelduck female (left) and male.*

The endemic paradise shelduck is well distributed throughout New Zealand, inhabiting wetlands, open pastures and streams in alpine regions. The birds are often seen in pairs in open country, the female being conspicuous with her white head. After the breeding season, they assemble into small flocks, flying in a 'V' formation. Males honk with a repeated 'Zoonk' call, but the female call is higher pitched. During the moulting period, paradise shelduck move from their territories to form large flocks on small lakes. After gaining their new plumage, pairs return to their natal territories, with birds pairing for life. The birds begin nesting in July and August in northern districts, but later in the south. Some pairs nest as late as December, presumably after losing their earlier clutch from predation. The female incubates the clutch of six to 10 eggs while the male guards the territory. Most nest sites are in hollows of fallen trees or in shallow burrows beneath exposed roots of large trees. In the north, nests are sometimes formed in holes of old puriri trees. Like grey ducks, they occasionally build nests in the fork of a tree. After hatching, ducklings are led to the water, often to quite small farm dams. They are guarded by the parents and if the group is disturbed while feeding on pasture, the ducklings run to the water, often diving to hide. The parents attempt to distract the intruder by leading it away from the area. When ducklings are about two months old they have developed a dark plumage, similar to that of the male, with females then gradually showing a white head.

An endemic, threatened species, the blue duck inhabits turbulent streams and rivers in high country throughout much of New Zealand. However, they are not found north of the central North Island. Their favourite habitats are alpine streams bordered by trees. Blue duck are the only duck species likely to be seen in these areas, apart from the occasional paradise shelduck. The birds are usually seen in pairs, and occupy the same stretch of river throughout the year. Blue duck are well camouflaged when resting on rocks, though their light-coloured bill reveals the bird's presence when it moves its head. An unusual feature is the soft, fleshy border to the bill, probably for protection as the bird feeds on invertebrates which often cling to underwater rocks. Caddis fly larvae are a favourite item in their diet, as well as insects and grubs that fall from overhanging trees. The birds are usually silent, but males give a high-pitched whistle and females call with a rasping note when disturbed. Blue ducks nest from early August, choosing a small cave, hollow log, beneath overhanging rocks or in thick vegetation. Nests are composed of vegetation and small sticks, then lined with grasses and feathers. The four to eight creamy-coloured eggs are incubated by the female for about five weeks. The ducklings are able to swim and dive soon after hatching, navigating the turbulent waters with their parents. When able to fly, they disperse to other areas, usually in the same river catchment.

**Mallard** *Anas platyrhynchos* 58 cm

*Mallard female (left) and male.*

The very common mallard was introduced to New Zealand for game purposes. They are now very well populated throughout the country, inhabiting wetlands, some marine estuaries and mudflats as well as urban areas. The drake has a strikingly coloured plumage in contrast to the drab, overall brown colouration of the female. However, they interbreed with some domestic species, producing various colourations. They also interbreed with the native grey duck. Grey duck and female mallard appear somewhat similar but the wing speculum is green in the grey duck and purple in the mallard. As well, the legs of the mallard are orange-coloured. In northern districts mallard often begin nesting in June. The nest, composed of grasses and lined generously with down, is concealed in dense vegetation close to water. The large clutch of up to 12 or more eggs is incubated by the female for four weeks. The chicks are taken to water soon after hatching, but unlike other duck species, the drakes do not usually accompany the ducklings. Mallard feed mainly by dabbling for water plants and on seeds, by upending in shallow water. They also graze waterside grasses and seeds from growing plants. To provide sufficient protein for egg laying, the female feeds on aquatic insects and other invertebrates, especially earthworms.

# Grey duck *Anas superciliosa* 55 cm

The native grey duck inhabits wetlands, being mainly small lakes and slow-flowing rivers. Unlike the common mallard, with which it interbreeds, it is uncommon in urban areas. It is more frequently seen in northern regions than in the south. The sexes are similar in appearance and somewhat resemble the female mallard. However, the grey duck has a darker plumage with a prominent dark eye stripe. The feet are greyish brown and the wing speculum is green, compared with the mallard's purple speculum. Birds that interbreed with mallard often differ in that their legs are a yellow colour. The feeding habits of the grey duck are similar to those of the mallard, taking vegetation, seeds and invertebrates. Nesting usually begins in June in northern districts and later in the south. A nest of grasses, lined with down, is concealed on thick vegetation, often some distance from water. Some nests are built in forks or holes of trees. The female incubates a clutch of six to 12 eggs for four weeks. The ducklings are so light in weight that they are uninjured if they fall from tree nests, several metres above ground.

**New Zealand shoveler** *Anas rhynchotis* 48 cm

*New Zealand shoveler: male (top); female (bottom).*

The New Zealand shoveler inhabits lowland swamps, lagoons and the shallow edges of lakes. Particularly in the shooting season, it often shelters in marine harbours. The shoveler is the fastest flying duck, showing its conspicuous white wing bars when in flight. Its wedge-shaped bill is equipped with lamellae along the edges, a feature enabling it to filter small food items from the water. Shovelers eat seeds, aquatic plants, insects, earthworms and water snails. Females are brownish in colour and at a distance resemble a female mallard. Males in breeding plumage are attractively coloured with a distinctive white crescent at the base of the bill. Shovelers sit low in the water, and do not appear as buoyant as mallards. Shovelers nest from August to October. The nest of grasses lined with down is concealed in thick vegetation, particularly tussock or sedges, often built some distance from water. As with other ducks, the female incubates the clutch, consisting of eight to 12 very pale blue eggs. Incubation takes three and a half weeks. The ducklings are taken to feed at the water's edge, often at night, hiding in lakeside vegetation during the day. Ducklings disperse when about two months old and often travel some distance from their natal habitat. Shovelers are rarely seen on suburban lakes.

## Grey teal *Anas gracilis* 43 cm

The grey teal inhabits lagoons, swamps and estuaries, preferring waters banked with a growth of vegetation. It is a very mobile duck and many are thought to have arrived in recent years from Australia, where they are common. They fly with a rapid wingbeat, and in flight show a prominent white triangle on the upper wing. Grey teal feed on seeds and aquatic invertebrates which they filter when dabbling in ooze and shallow water. They also upend to take food from the bottom of shallow ponds. A clutch of five to eight eggs is laid from June to November, in a nest built of grasses, in tree hollows, burrows or clumps of sedges. Acclimatisation societies provide nest boxes on posts in wetland areas, which the birds readily accept for use.

## Brown teal *Anas aucklandica* 48 cm

The brown teal is an endangered endemic species. It was common in wetlands, rivers and tidal estuaries, but due to vegetation being cleared from river banks and predation by stoats, the teal is now endangered. Brown teal feed mainly at dusk and dawn, hiding in bankside undergrowth during the day. The main population now inhabits wetlands on Great Barrier Island,  with a few flocks on tidal estuaries of the east coast of Northland. A small population survives in parts of Fiordland. Brown teal breed successfully in captivity, with some then being released into the wild. They breed naturally by building nests of grasses in thick vegetation, close to water. Females incubate a clutch of four to six eggs for four weeks. Nesting begins in June and many nests are found as late as March.

## New Zealand scaup *Aythya novaeseelandiae* 40 cm

*New Zealand scaup: male (top); female (bottom).*

The endemic New Zealand scaup, or black teal, is the only true diving duck and also the smallest duck. It inhabits mainly deep clear-water lakes throughout the country, but is also found on many of the dune lakes of Northland. It is absent from the off-shore islands. New Zealand scaup are most common on the Rotorua lakes, Lake Taupo, the Waikato hydroelectric lakes and many of the subalpine lakes of the South Island. They dive from the surface when feeding, and can remain submerged for more than 40 seconds. Most dives last for about 15 seconds. The birds feed on aquatic invertebrates and water plants. In autumn they congregate in flocks with some flocks consisting only of male birds, recognised by their golden-coloured eye. Scaup fly rapidly, revealing their white underwing. In late winter the flocks break up to form pairs. The female builds a nest of grasses lined with down, in sedges and thick waterside undergrowth. She incubates the clutch of five to 10 eggs for 28 to 30 days. The ducklings are able to dive immediately after hatching and, although they stay with the parent, catch their own food.

# Australasian harrier *Circus approximans* 55–60 cm

Australasian harriers are common, inhabiting coastal areas, wetlands, open agricultural country, forest margins and subalpine tussock. As with diurnal raptors, the female is larger than the male. Birds are a deep brown when young but, as they age, progressively become paler in plumage colour, some appearing almost grey. Harriers are frequently seen quartering the ground in a leisurely flight interspersed with glides. Unlike the falcon, they do not strike their prey in the air, but glide slowly then suddenly drop on their prey. They feed on carrion, particularly possums, rabbits and hedgehogs killed on the road. They also feed on a variety of live prey, including rabbits, birds, lizards, frogs, large insects and occasional fish. They have been reported as taking bird's eggs and their young from open nests. Pairing begins in winter, when the birds soar high in the air, performing courtship diving and calling with a high-pitched, repeated 'kee-kee' whistle. Nest building begins in early August in northern districts. Bulky structures composed of sticks, raupo and grasses are usually sited in raupo swamps, among sedges, in long grass, and sometimes in crowns of treeferns. The clutch of four or five eggs is laid at two-day intervals. Incubation, by the female only, begins with the laying of the first egg. The chick when hatched after incubation of four and a half weeks is disproportionate in size, with only the larger two or three chicks surviving. The chicks are fed by the female, but the male harrier does most of the hunting, bringing food to the female while she is incubating and after the chicks hatch.

## New Zealand falcon *Falco novaeseelandiae* 43–47 cm

The endemic New Zealand falcon is easily distinguished from the harrier by its direct flight, with rapid beats of its long, pointed wings. It often perches on prominent rocks or treetops, waiting to swoop on prey. New Zealand falcons are not common, but are most likely to be seen in high country on the eastern side of the Southern Alps. Some inhabit forested areas throughout New Zealand. The forest race are darker in colour, with more rounded wings than those inhabiting open country. Unlike harriers, New Zealand falcons do not normally feed on carrion. They strike with their talons, after a direct swooping flight, to catch young rabbits and ground-dwelling birds, also striking other birds in mid-air. Introduced finches form a large proportion of their diet. The call of the falcon is a repeated 'kek-kek-kek' and sometimes a scream. They are extremely aggressive, particularly in protection of their nests. At this time they will attack humans or animals approaching within 100 m or more of their nesting territory. Unlike the hawks, falcons use no materials to furnish their nests. They make a slight depression in the ground under a rock ledge or under a log and sometimes on the ground in an exotic fire break. The bush race of falcons nest in clumps of astelia high in trees. The usual clutch consists of three or four buff-coloured, russet-brown marked eggs. Both sexes take turns at incubation and chicks hatch after 30 to 33 days. The smaller male chicks fledge at 32 days old, and the larger female chicks at 35 days.

## California quail *Callipepla californica* 25 cm

California quail were introduced to New Zealand in the 1860s for game purposes. They are common in most open country areas throughout New Zealand. They are usually seen in family groups and, after the nesting season, the birds congregate in large coveys. When disturbed, they fly rapidly with whirring wingbeats. They sometimes venture into gardens in country districts, in search of food. California quail feed on a variety of seeds, succulent plants and insects, and also on some fruit. Nesting begins in early September, in a nest of grasses, hidden in rough scrub. Often nests are built under gorse or manuka that has been felled. Large clutches of 10 to 18 cream-coloured eggs are laid and incubated by the female for 23 days. The eggs all hatch within three or four hours and the chicks leave the nest soon after they are dry. They are accompanied by both parents, but are able to feed themselves. When a family is disturbed, it is surprising to see the chicks, not fully feathered, but able to fly.

## Chukor *Alectoris chukar* 33 cm

Chukor were introduced to New Zealand in the 1920s from Pakistan and Iran. Some birds are seen in the Bay of Plenty and Hawke's Bay, but the main population inhabits the dry, high country east of the Southern Alps and commonly the tussock country. Populations have also settled in the high country of Marlborough and the Nelson Lakes National Park. Like quail, chukor feed on seeds, succulent foliage and fallen berries. Insects are also eaten, particularly by the chicks. Nests are composed of grasses hidden under overhanging rocks, or in thick vegetation. The female incubates the large clutch of up to 20 eggs, for 24 days. Chicks leave the nest within a few hours of hatching and accompany the parents, but feed themselves.

**Brown quail** *Synoicus ypsilophorus* 18 cm

Brown quail were introduced from Tasmania, and perhaps Australia, in the 1860s. They are the smallest quail found in New Zealand, somewhat resembling the endemic New Zealand quail, which became extinct in the 1800s. Brown quail are reasonably common in Northland and Tiritiri Matangi Island. A few birds are seen in the Bay of Plenty. They inhabit scrub and rough pastures, where they feed on seeds, succulent foliage, fallen fruits and a few insects. Nesting extends from August to December. A nest of dry grasses is built on the ground, hidden in dense herbage. The usual clutch consists of up to 12 cream-coloured, brown-speckled eggs. The female incubates for three weeks and, like other game birds, the chicks leave the nest with the parents, soon after hatching.

**Ring-necked pheasant** *Phasianus colchicus* 60–80 cm

Several introductions of pheasants have been made to New Zealand for game purposes since the mid-1800s. Apart from breeding in the wild, some birds are reared in captivity and released into the wild. The female is an overall brown colour and has a shorter tail than the cock bird (illustrated). Except for the Nelson district, pheasants are uncommon in the South Island. In the North Island they are widely distributed, inhabiting open farmland and scrub country. They feed mainly on seeds, succulent foliage, fruit and sometimes insects. The nest of dried grasses is built in thick vegetation, often among growing crops and hayfields. Up to 14 olive-green eggs are laid from September onwards, incubated by the female for just over three weeks.

## Banded rail *Rallus philippensis* 30 cm

The secretive banded rail inhabits mangrove swamps and sedge-covered salt marshes. It is also found on inland freshwater wetlands and may follow small streams into farmlands. Except for coastal regions of north-west Nelson and parts of the Marlborough Sounds, they are uncommon in the South Island. The main population is located on coastal areas of Northland, Great Barrier Island and the Bay of Plenty. Banded rails prefer seclusion, with the usual view of the bird being of it running rapidly to the shelter of mangroves, when disturbed feeding along a tidal creek. They rarely take to the air, although the birds are able to fly well. Food consists chiefly of marine crustaceans, crabs, insects and earthworms. Banded rails have a very extended nesting season. In the north, nesting begins in July or August, and nests may be found as late as March. These could be a second brood, but as nests are often predated by rats, the late nests may be due to earlier losses. The most common nesting sites are in sedges that back mangrove forests. Dry sedges and grasses form a nest, with sedges bent over to form a bower and conceal the nest from avian predators. Two to five buff-coloured eggs with brown markings are incubated for three weeks by both sexes. Chicks, which are covered in sooty coloured down, leave the nest and feed when a day old, being guarded by the parents for nine to 10 weeks.

## Weka *Gallirallus australis* 53 cm

Four subspecies of the endemic, flightless weka have settled in various regions of New Zealand. The buff weka became extinct in the South Island, but is very common in the Chathams where it was introduced. Due to predation and possibly disease, the weka population has declined rapidly in the North Island since the 1930s. They survive on some offshore islands, such as Kapiti and Kawau Islands. The birds have bred successfully in captivity, but after liberation into the wild they face elimination by predation from stoats. Although weka have wings which are reasonably developed, they are flightless. The birds run rapidly, and although not web-footed, they are able to swim long distances. This has been proved when removed from an island; their strong homing instinct enabled them to swim back, over at least a kilometre of water. Weka enjoy a varied diet, feeding usually on invertebrates, lizards, fruits, seeds and foliage. They also catch mice and rob eggs and young birds from nests, even taking petrel chicks from nesting burrows. The weka's nesting season is an extended one, with peak periods from September to December. Two to five cream-coloured, brown-marked eggs are laid in a nest composed of grasses, hidden in thick herbage or under a fallen log. Both sexes incubate for three and a half weeks. Chicks are covered in sooty-coloured down and can run and feed soon after leaving the nest.

**Spotless crake** *Porzana tabuensis* 20 cm

This tiny rail is common in swamps throughout New Zealand. Even very small borders of raupo swamp may harbour a pair. Spotless crake are extremely secretive, and usually feed at dawn and late in the day. However, if a tape recording of their calls is played, the birds will respond at any time of the day, often creeping to open view. Their main diet consists of insects and their larvae, tadpoles and earthworms. The usual nest site is in a clump of the small, bright-green cutty grass in a raupo swamp. Some nests are sited about a metre above water level and others lower down. Spotless crake nest as early as July in the northern areas. Both sexes incubate the clutch of two or three buff-coloured, brown-spotted eggs. Incubation takes three weeks. Chicks, covered with a sooty down, stay in the nest for two or three days and later feed with the parents under thick cover. The closely related **marsh crake**, ***Porzana pusilla***, is less common, particularly in the North Island. In the South Island it frequents lake edges with a bordering of vegetation. They nest in clumps of sedges close to the water. Both the spotless and marsh crakes possess strong homing instincts, and in some cases where birds are relocated, due to drainage of a swamp, they will fly back to their usual habitat, presumably flying at night.

63

## Pukeko *Porphyrio porphyrio* 51 cm

This cosmopolitan species, which is common in Australia and South Africa, is widely distributed in wetter locations of New Zealand. Pukeko inhabit lagoons, swamps, pastures with clumps of rushes and city parks. The birds are also seen feeding along verges of busy roads and motorways. In some areas, birds are seen in pairs, often with two or three chicks. In other territories they live in communities of several birds, some adult, others immature and others chicks. Although not web-footed, they are frequently seen swimming and in spite of appearing clumsy in flight, pukeko can fly long distances. The varied diet consists of vegetation, with the stems being held in one foot (parrot fashion), invertebrates and frogs. They also rob eggs from ground-nesting birds and damage crops, uprooting corn seedlings as well as taking other vegetables. Pukeko nest over an extended season. Although nests may be found during many months of the year, most nesting occurs between August and December. Single pairs nest in raupo swamps, in thick foliage or in clumps of rushes on rough farm paddocks. In communities two or three females will lay eggs in one nest and several members of the extended family take turns at incubation and feeding of the chicks. Some of the community nests may contain up to 12 eggs. Incubation takes about 24 days, and although chicks can walk soon after hatching, they stay in or around the nest for the first few days after hatching.

## South Island takahe *Porphyrio mantelli* 63 cm

The takahe is the world's largest rail. This endangered endemic bird was thought to be extinct, until rediscovered by Dr Orbell in the Muchison Mountain region of Fiordland in 1948. The present wild population is around 120 birds, their numbers being limited by predation from stoats. In winter, when their usual feeding grounds are snow-covered, the birds move to stands of beech forest in the adjacent valleys. However, red deer compete for food in these environments. Some takahe have been transferred to predator-free islands, such as Kapiti, Mana and Tiritiri Matangi islands. Here they can be viewed at close quarters and are breeding with some success. Captive birds are being successfully reared at the Mount Bruce and Te Anau wildlife centres. Chicks that survive to adulthood are liberated in the Stuart Mountain region of Fiordland. In the wild takahe feed mainly on the stems of snow tussock leaves and, in their winter habitats, their main food consists of the rhizomes of ferns. On their island homes, they feed on a wide variety of grasses and fallen fruits from shrubs. In the wild, nesting takes place in October and November. The nest is composed of dried tussock stems and grasses. The usual clutch consists of two eggs, incubated by both sexes for about four weeks. However, invariably only one chick survives.

## Australian coot *Fulica atra* 38 cm

The Australian coot introduced itself to New Zealand in 1958, where the bird was first seen on Lake Hayes in the South Island. It bred successfully and spread to inhabit freshwater lakes throughout the country. Coots prefer clear-water lakes, fringed with raupo or rushes which provide suitable nesting sites. They are frequently seen in many urban parks mingling with ducks, and receiving food items offered or left by humans. Coots are the most aquatic of the rails, only coming to land to rest or nest. They are strong fliers and migrate to other stretches of water after nesting, where they form large flocks. The birds feed mainly on succulent water plants and invertebrates. They make shallow dives, seldom remaining submerged for more than 10 seconds. Coots are aggressive when nesting or accompanying their chicks, even chasing birds as large as black swans from their territory. Nests can be found during many months of the year in northern districts, but peak nesting occurs between August and December. Coots usually raise two or three broods in a season. Nests, built close to the water, are substantial structures composed of stems of rushes and raupo. Four to six cream-coloured, dark-spotted eggs are incubated by both sexes for three weeks. The chicks remain in the nest for a few days after hatching, making short sorties to swim and be fed by the parents.

## South Island pied oystercatcher
*Haematopus ostralegus* 46 cm

Several species of oystercatcher inhabit many countries throughout the world. They are numerous and increasing in numbers in New Zealand. South Island pied oystercatchers, usually referred to as 'Sipo', nest only in the South Island but non-breeding birds are common in the North Island throughout the year. They inhabit tidal estuaries, mudflats and sheltered beaches where they often occur in large flocks. During the nesting season the birds inhabit inland areas of the South Island, feeding and nesting in farm pastures, cultivated grounds and in subalpine regions. Their bills are adapted for probing earthworms, insect larvae, marine crustaceans and bivalve shellfish. The last are often inserted in an upright position in the sand or mud and then prised open to retrieve the contents. 'Sipo' are distinguished from the pied forms of the larger variable oystercatcher by their slimmer build and uniform pied marking. The oystercatchers are thought to pair for life and nest only in the South Island, although a recent nesting was reported from Hawke's Bay. Shingle riverbeds, ploughed paddocks and pastures are the favoured nesting sites. Nests are a mere scraped depression in the ground, where two or three buff-coloured, brown-marked eggs are laid between August and October. Both sexes share incubation for four weeks, and chicks leave the nest two or three days after hatching.

**Variable oystercatcher** *Haematopus unicolor* 48 cm

The variable oystercatcher is endemic to New Zealand, and is the only oystercatcher that is polymorphic and shows plumage colour variations, from pied to black. The black plumage forms are more common in the south, particularly on Stewart Island. Variable oystercatchers inhabit coastal environments and are not found inland. They are usually seen in pairs on sandy beaches and spits, but in winter months they gather in small flocks of up to 50 or more birds, to feed in sheltered marine estuaries and harbours. They are a threatened species and are far less common than the 'Sipo'. The bird feeds by probing deeply in shallow water, sand and mud to extract marine worms, molluscs and larger bivalve shells. These are often placed upright in the sand and prised open to draw out the contents. Variable oystercatchers begin courtship in early spring in the north and a little later in the south. The nest is a scrape in the sand, usually well above high water and often partly concealed under dune vegetation. Where birds nest on rocky shores, the nest is a scrape in the sand between rocks. The clutch of two or three very large eggs is laid between September and December. The eggs are buff-coloured with numerous dark-brown markings. Both sexes share incubation, which lasts for four weeks. Newly hatched chicks are covered with pepper-coloured down. They leave the nest when two days old and are able to fly after six or seven weeks.

# Pied stilt *Himantopus himantopus* 35 cm

Subspecies of the pied stilt inhabit many countries of the world where habitats are suitable. Overseas they are known as black-winged stilts. In New Zealand the pied stilt is very common in freshwater wetlands, tidal estuaries, marine mudflats and harbours and, particularly in winter months, on wet pastures. Their numbers are increasing, yet they are uncommon on Stewart Island and offshore islands. Pied stilts feed on a wide range of insects and their larvae, earthworms, marine molluscs and crustaceans. Their feeding behaviour varies with the actual habitat. They probe in soft soil and marine mudflats, they sweep their bills sideways in ooze and shallow water, and they pick insects from the water surface while wading. In strong winds they sometimes stand still in shallow water, waiting, as organisms are blown along the surface of the water, which they then quickly grasp with their bills. Pied stilts begin nesting in July. These early nests usually form part of a loose colony in swampy paddocks or at the edges of ponds. Later nesting is located on shellbanks, shingle riverbeds or sometimes on sand dunes. Most clutches contain four heavily marked, fawn-coloured eggs. Both sexes incubate for three and a half weeks, with the chicks leaving the nest soon after hatching.

69

# Black stilt *Himantopus novaezelandiae* 38 cm

The endemic, highly endangered black stilt is the world's rarest wader. The wild population, mainly inhabiting the Waitaki River catchment in the South Island, numbers approximately 120 birds. Others are captive in some Department of Conservation breeding centres. Black stilts are usually seen singly or in small groups. They have not developed the same cautious, protective instincts as the pied stilt, so are more readily subject to predation by stoats and feral cats. The birds generally feed in small freshwater lagoons and on deltas where some rivers flow

*Hybrid black stilt.*

into the larger lakes. Black stilts feed on a variety of aquatic insects and their larvae as well as earthworms. After the nesting season some birds migrate to a few marine harbours in the North Island. Also frequently seen in these locations are hybrid birds. These are the result of isolated black stilts pairing with pied stilts. Hybrid birds show white underparts and facial markings. Nesting begins in September, and unlike pied stilts, black stilts nest in isolation, leaving them particularly vulnerable to predation, as they do not receive warnings from other birds. Three or four buff-coloured, dark brown-marked eggs are laid in a nest of grasses in a scrape in fine shingle of a riverbed. Other nests are located on small river islands or on the banks of ponds in swamps. Incubation is shared by the sexes, taking about 25 days, and like the pied stilt, chicks are active soon after hatching.

# New Zealand dotterel *Charadrius obscurus* 27 cm

This threatened, endemic dotterel settles on sandy coasts, marine harbours and estuaries. Apart from a small habitation on the Gisborne coast, the northern subspecies forms the main population, and is only found north of the eastern Bay of Plenty and Raglan on the west coast. The Stewart Island subspecies is a slightly larger bird, with a brighter plumage. It is confined to a small population on Stewart Island, where they inhabit high country during the nesting season, then migrate to marine estuaries and mudflats, with some birds moving to the Southland coast. The Stewart Island residents have been reduced by feral cat predation, with the northern birds suffering predation by stoats and cats, and hedgehogs taking eggs. In summer, nests are disturbed or destroyed by four-wheel drive vehicles and domestic dogs. However, in recent years, predator control and fencing of nesting areas are helping to increase dotterel numbers. New Zealand dotterels feed on a wide range of marine invertebrates, particularly sandhoppers. When feeding on mudflats, they often catch crabs. The Stewart Island birds also eat earthworms. In the north, nesting takes place between August and December. Three buff-coloured, brown-marked eggs are laid in a scrape in the sand, close to a piece of driftwood, or partly hidden in dune vegetation. Females incubate during the day and males at night. Chicks hatch after four weeks and are active soon after hatching.

71

**Banded dotterel** *Charadrius bicinctus* 20 cm

The common, endemic banded dotterel inhabits coastal beaches and coastal pastures, mudflats, shingle riverbeds and high country. The birds also reside in the inhospitable Rangipo Desert. After the breeding season, many of the South Island birds migrate to coastal Tasmania and Australia, and those in the northern regions of the South Island move to the North Island, mainly to coastal estuaries and harbours, where they form large flocks. Banded dotterels feed on marine invertebrates and freshwater insects and their larvae. In wet pastures they take earthworms. The birds have also been observed eating small fruits of plant foliage. Their nesting season in northern areas begins in early August, and in all regions nests may be found as late as January. The usual clutch consists of three buff-coloured, dark brown blotch-marked eggs. The nest is a scrape in the ground, in sand, among river shingle and on short grass paddocks. The female performs most of the incubation during the day, and the male at night. But the behaviour is not regular and the birds often change shifts during the day. Banded dotterels are far more wary during the nesting season than New Zealand dotterels, and their nests are often very difficult to find. Incubation takes just under four weeks, and the cryptically coloured chicks are active soon after hatching. After the nesting season, birds lose their distinctive double breast bands, and may be confused with some of the migrant waders.

## Black-fronted dotterel *Charadrius melanops* 18 cm

*Black-fronted dotterel, one-day-old chicks.*

This Australian species introduced itself to the shingle rivers in southern Hawke's Bay in the 1950s. They bred successfully and have now spread to other shingle rivers in the lower North Island as well as several rivers in the eastern South Island. After nesting, many form small groups, feeding in wetlands, the edges of lagoons and some estuaries. However, most birds remain on the riverbeds, while a few vagrants are seen in the northern North Island. The colourful black-fronted dotterel is the smallest of the native plovers and is easily recognised by its small size, bright red bill and conspicuous black V-shaped band across its white chest. When disturbed by humans the birds crouch with their back to the observer, making them difficult to locate among the shingle. The birds feed mainly on aquatic crustaceans, insects and earthworms. From August to December, the black-fronted dotterel nests, making a scrape in the shingle, often near driftwood. The nest scrape is usually decorated with small pieces of driftwood and small stones, with sometimes a little dried grass lining the nest. The three buff-coloured, darkly marked eggs are incubated by both sexes for three weeks. The chicks are active soon after hatching.

73

**Wrybill** *Anarhynchus frontalis* 20 cm

The endemic wrybill is unique in that the tip of its bill twists to the right. It is thought that this feature enables the birds to more readily capture insects from beneath river stones. The birds, with their cryptic colouring, match the colour of the riverbed stones, and unless they move, are very difficult to see. Wrybills are most readily observed when they migrate to North Island mudflats and harbours. Here, they may be easily approached where they have formed tight flocks. The birds are a striking sight as, in a tightly grouped flock, they fly above feeding grounds, twisting and turning with the light reflecting from their silvery plumage. Wrybills feed on insects and their larvae, particularly caddis fly larvae. When rivers are in flood, the birds feed along the riverbanks. Their diet also consists of marine crustaceans and aquatic insects. In shallow pools and ooze, they feed by swinging their bills from side to side in a scything fashion, to capture marine organisms. From August to December, the birds nest only on the shingle braided rivers on the eastern side of the Southern Alps. Here they make a scrape in shingle between large stones, laying two eggs, the colour matching exactly the riverbed stones. No nesting material is used, and sexes share incubation for four weeks. The chicks are active within a few hours of hatching. Later nests may be a second brood, or due to the loss of an earlier nest by flooding or predation.

## Pacific golden plover *Pluvialis fulva* 25 cm

*Pacific golden plover, breeding plumage.*

After nesting in the tundra, the main population of Pacific golden plover migrate south to spend the northern winter on the coasts of southern Asia. However, approximately 1000 birds reach New Zealand and spread as far south as Southland. They frequent many harbours and estuaries, sometimes feeding on coastal pastures where their main diet consists of earthworms. The larger **grey plover**, ***Pluvialis squatarola***, visits New Zealand in very small numbers. Their feeding habits differ from the golden plover, as they usually feed close to the tideline of estuaries, often by wading. Both species feed on a range of marine crustaceans, molluscs and insects. The golden plover breeds in central and eastern Siberia and Alaska. The grey plover breeds over an area extending from northern Canada to central Siberia.

## Spur-winged plover *Vanellus miles* 38 cm

The Australian spur-winged plover introduced itself to Southland in the 1930s. They bred successfully and have spread throughout New Zealand, inhabiting open country and farm pastures, particularly where there are ponds or small streams. They are also found on the shorelines of lakes, lagoons and on sheltered coasts. Spur-winged plovers are easily recognised by their flopping lapwing flight and their loud, high-pitched rattling call. Farmers consider the birds beneficial, as they feed on grass grubs and other insect pests. However, they are predatory on the nests of other ground-nesting birds. Plovers also feed on earthworms, and in coastal regions eat crustaceans and aquatic insects. The birds have an extended nesting season and often rear two or more broods in a season. Nesting begins in June through to March. The nest is a scrape in the ground in a ploughed field or pasture. Little or no nesting material is used, except when nesting on shingle, where small sticks and grasses are added. The usual clutch consists of three or four brown, darkly blotched eggs. Incubation is shared by the sexes, taking just over four weeks. Chicks are active soon after hatching and peck for themselves while accompanying parents.

# Migrants

Each summer, from late September, tens of thousands of waders, having just completed nesting in the tundra regions of Siberia and Alaska, visit New Zealand's harbours and estuaries. They arrive thin, drab and underweight, after this long migration, but gain weight through the summer months here, feeding on the rich larders of the mudflats and sandy estuaries. By far the best known and most numerous of these migrants are the bar-tailed godwits, with over 100,000 arriving on these shores each summer. The next most numerous are the red knot, or lesser knot, whose numbers reach 60,000. These two species far outnumber the ruddy turnstones and several species of sandpiper and plover. The smallest of these migrants is the red-necked stint, a bird the size of the common house sparrow. These very tiny birds have the ability to navigate thousands of kilometres, much of this distance over oceans, to spend the summer feeding here. Most of these migrants put on weight, moult their old feathers with some assuming a colourful nuptial plumage, before flying back to nest near the Arctic Circle. However, some young and non-breeding birds remain throughout the winter in New Zealand.

*Waders mobbing before migrating.*

### Eastern curlew *Numenius madagascariensis* 63 cm

The eastern curlew is the largest of the migrant waders, being twice the size of the godwit and easily distinguished by its long, decurved bill. They are extremely wary, and when approached as they roost near a flock of godwits, they will fly off before the godwits even become restless. The curlew's very long bill enables it to probe deeply in soft mud to catch marine worms. It also feeds on a wide range of marine crustaceans, especially mud crabs. It nests in the tundra regions of Siberia.

### Asiatic whimbrel *Numenius phaeopus* 43 cm

The asiatic whimbrel is about the same size as the godwit but can be recognised by its shorter, decurved bill. Like the eastern curlew, it is very wary, and when approached as birds roost near a flock of godwits, they will fly off before the godwits even become restless. The asiatic whimbrel feeds on a wide range of marine crustaceans, especially mud crabs. It nests in the tundra regions of Siberia.

## Bar-tailed godwit *Limosa lapponica* 40 cm

Bar-tailed godwits are the most numerous of the Arctic migrant waders to visit New Zealand each summer. Banding of godwits has shown that most birds come from Siberia and others from Alaska. Their numbers in New Zealand exceed 100,000 distributed in many harbours and sheltered coasts throughout the country. They are usually seen feeding in flocks along the tideline or probing for marine worms, crustaceans and molluscs in soft mud. As the tide rises, they progressively move from these feeding grounds, to roost in tightly packed flocks on shellbanks, sandspits or standing in shallow water lagoons. Most birds leave for their northern hemisphere nesting grounds in late March or early April. However, as many as 10,000 young birds remain on the feeding grounds in New Zealand during the winter months.

**Lesser knot (Red knot)** *Calidris canutus* 24 cm

The lesser, or red, knot forms the second largest number of migrant waders to visit New Zealand. Some 60,000 birds migrate to the harbours and estuaries, and about 5000 birds overwinter, mainly in the Manukau and Kaipara harbours. Knots feed on a wide variety of marine crustaceans, molluscs and thin-shelled bivalves. As they have shorter bills than godwits or curlews, they probe for marine food that is not so deeply wedged in the mud-flat, so the birds do not compete for food with other waders. After their late summer moult, many birds, particularly males, assume a colourful russet nuptial plumage. Most of the lesser knots nest in the tundra regions of eastern Siberia.

**Turnstone** *Arenaria interpres* 23 cm

Approximately 6000 turnstones migrate to New Zealand after nesting in eastern Siberia and Alaska. They form the third largest population of Arctic waders to migrate here. Turnstones are easily recognised, as their plumage colour is unlike any other wader. They are active when feeding, turning over shells, small stones and pieces of driftwood to seek out sandhoppers and other inverte-brates. Turnstones are usually seen in small flocks and, when approached, do not fly off a few at a time, but suddenly take wing together. The birds nest above the Arctic Circle, in northern Siberia and Alaska.

Up to 200 sharp-tailed sandpipers migrate to New Zealand each year, and a few overwinter here. They usually inhabit saltmarshes, the upper shoreline of harbours and particularly coastal lagoons and small freshwater pools close to the shore. They often roost among flocks of wrybills or may be seen in small groups on beds of *Sarcocornia*, and sometimes with high-tide roosts of lesser knots. Sharp-tailed sandpipers feed on a variable diet of crustaceans, particularly sandhoppers, molluscs and aquatic insects and their larvae. They nest in the Arctic tundra of eastern Siberia, with a few records only of breeding in Alaska.

## Pectoral sandpiper *Calidris melanotos* 23 cm

Only small numbers of pectoral sandpipers visit New Zealand each summer. They can be distinguished from the sharp-tailed sandpiper, in their non-breeding plumage, by the more distinctive upper breast speckling and their less rufous plumage colouring. They also lack the boomerang-shaped brown markings on the sides of the breast, which are shown on the sharp-tailed sandpiper. Their feeding habitat also differs, as they favour coastal freshwater pools and lagoons. They may also be found on the shores of Lake Ellesmere in Canterbury. The birds feed mainly on freshwater aquatic insects and their larvae. As the main breeding grounds of the pectoral sandpiper are in northern Canada, Alaska and northern Siberia, most birds migrate to spend the southern hemisphere summer in South America.

## Curlew sandpiper *Calidris ferruginea* 22 cm

Curlew sandpipers are easily recognised by their decurved bill. When roosting at high tide, they frequently mix into flocks of wrybill. Up to 100 curlew sandpipers visit New Zealand each summer, and a few non-breeding birds overwinter here. The birds feed by deeply probing into soft mud to obtain marine worms, molluscs and crustaceans. They also take marine organisms from shallow saltwater pools. In late summer, before migrating to nest, they often assume a spectacular russet-coloured nuptial plumage. Their main breeding grounds are in the high latitude regions of central Siberia with some recorded as nesting in Alaska.

82

## Terek sandpiper *Tringa terek* 23 cm

Small numbers of terek sandpipers migrate to New Zealand each summer, inhabiting estuaries and mudflats. They are restless birds and, when feeding, move about suddenly in different directions. They usually mingle with flocks of wrybill at high-tide roosts, or sometimes with banded dotterel if wrybill are not present. Terek sandpipers are easily recognised by their long, upturned bill. Their greyish eclipse plumage changes in late summer to brownish, with speckled upper breast and bright yellow legs. When feeding, the birds probe deeply for marine worms, molluscs and crustaceans. They are often seen feeding on aquatic insects in shallow pools. Terek sandpipers nest in the tundra regions of the Arctic Circle, which extend from eastern Siberia to as far as Finland in the west.

## Red-necked stint *Calidris ruficollis* 15 cm

Up to 300 of these sparrow-sized waders visit New Zealand estuaries, harbours and coastal lagoons each summer, with tens of thousands visiting coastal habitats of Australia. These tiny birds endure the vast distance of this migration, much of the journey crossing large areas of ocean. Red-necked stints are easily recognised by their small size, short bill and, in autumn, their nuptial plumage of a russet-coloured head and neck, often referred to as a 'balaclava'. At high tide they roost with wrybills, sometimes sharp-tailed sandpipers or banded dotterels. Their favourite feeding sites are in shallow mud pools, where they collect marine organisms by rapidly pecking in a sewing-machine fashion. Red-necked stints nest in the tundra regions of Alaska and Siberia.

## Wandering tattler *Tringa incarna* 28 cm

A small number of wandering tattlers visit New Zealand coasts each year. They are difficult to distinguish from the Siberian tattler, but their habitat preference differs. Wandering tattlers prefer rocky shores and rock platforms, such as those at Kaikoura. When feeding on these rocky shores they dash to catch marine organisms as each wave recedes, then retreat rapidly again. They are also seen on some gravel beaches. When in autumn breeding plumage, the wandering tattler can be distinguished by the barred underparts, extending to the under-tail coverts. Also, when disturbed it flies off, calling with a rippling trill. It nests in eastern Siberia.

## Siberian (grey-tailed) tattler *Tringa brevipes* 25 cm

A small number of Siberian, or grey-tailed, tattlers visit New Zealand coasts each year. They are difficult to distinguish from the wandering tattler, but their habitat preference differs. The slightly smaller Siberian tattler prefers to feed on mudflats and tidal estuaries. They usually mingle with wrybill at high-tide roosts. The Siberian tattler calls with a high-pitched two-note whistle. Like the wandering tattler, it nests in eastern Siberia.

## Marsh sandpiper *Tringa stagnatilis* 22 cm

Only a few marsh sandpipers visit New Zealand each summer, with some being seen overwintering. Unlike many of the other migrant waders, they prefer brackish and freshwater habitats. Some are seen in the upper reaches of tidal estuaries, but most sightings are of birds feeding in freshwater or brackish coastal lagoons. They often associate with pied stilts. They are easily recognised by their long legs, slim build and their very active, graceful feeding habits. They eat a variety of crustaceans and insects and their larvae. Although associating with stilts, they are often chased away when encroaching on the stilt's feeding territory. Marsh sandpipers nest in wetland areas of the steppes of central Asia.

## Brown skua *Catharacta skua* 63 cm

Skuas are related to gulls, and in habit they are piratic, chasing terns and small gulls to force them to disgorge their food. The large brown skua inhabits the southern subantarctic islands, but can often be seen in the waters around Stewart Island where they breed on some of the offshore islands. In winter the birds are sometimes seen around the South Island coast. Brown skuas are aggressive birds and prey on the eggs and chicks of other seabirds, and, in particular, take petrels at night. They also feed on carrion and fish.

## Arctic skua *Stercorarius parasiticus* 43 cm

The arctic skua is the most commonly observed skua in New Zealand waters, notably in the Hauraki Gulf. After nesting in the northern hemisphere tundra regions, the birds begin to arrive in New Zealand in November. Arctic skuas appear somewhat similar to an immature black-backed gull, but their flight is more purposeful, with a more jerky wingbeat. The plumage colour of most birds seen in New Zealand waters is a dark brown, but a few show lighter barred underparts and light-coloured wings. During the breeding season arctic skuas display long tail streamers, but the birds seen in coastal waters here have usually moulted these feathers. More rarely seen in New Zealand waters is the larger, stocky **pomarine skua**, *Stercorarius pomarinus*. This bird sometimes retains the twisted feathers which project beyond the tail. Both the arctic skua and the pomarine skua aerobatically chase red-billed gulls and white-fronted terns, forcing them to disgorge their freshly caught fish, which is taken in mid-air by the skuas.

## Black-backed gull *Larus dominicanus* 60 cm

*Black-backed gull, immature.*

Also known as the Dominican gull, the black-backed gull, which is the largest of New Zealand's three species of gull, is very common around all the coasts. It is also found inland around lakes, rivers, pastures, newly ploughed fields and some alpine habitats. They may be seen scavenging on urban rubbish dumps. Adult black-backed gulls are easily recognised, but the juvenile and immature birds differ in colour from the adults. Juveniles are brown with a mottled breast and lightly edged feathers. In their second year, the breast becomes white, flecked with brown and the upper wings and back become a darker brown. In their third year the birds almost resemble adults, except for a dark tip to the tail feathers and the upper wings are not entirely black. Black-backed gulls feed on fish, carrion, marine invertebrates, and sheep placentae. They also rob eggs from other ground-nesting birds. When feeding on shellfish, they drop them from a height to break them open. In August, birds congregate to nest in loose colonies among sand dunes, on boulder banks, shellspits or on rocky shores. However, many black-backed gull pairs nest in isolation on grassy headlands, small rocky islets, on the roof tops of industrial buildings and inland in the high country. Two or three buff-coloured, darkly marked eggs are laid from early September to late December in a nest composed of seaweed and grasses. Both sexes incubate for four weeks. Chicks remain in or close to the nest for several days and are fed on regurgitated food.

**Red-billed gull** *Larus novaehollandiae* 37 cm

*Red-billed gull, immature.*

The red-billed gull, known as the silver gull in Australia, is very common around New Zealand coasts. The bird also ventures some distance inland in stormy weather, to feed on earthworms in wet paddocks, parks and school playing fields. In summer months, red-billed gulls feed on small marine fish, often in association with white-fronted terns and shearwaters. In shallow pools within estuaries and mudflats, they often paddle in one spot to bring marine organisms to the surface. Their diet changes in winter months when they feed on shoreline carrion, marine invertebrates and offal from fishing vessels. They congregate in large colonies to nest in early spring, choosing shellbanks and offshore rocky islets. The largest mainland colony is at Kaikoura on the east coast of the South Island. Here, 5000 pairs nest each year in association with a nesting colony of white-fronted terns. An inland colony on the edge of Lake Rotorua shares a nesting site with the endemic black-billed gulls. Other large colonies exist on some offshore islands. The nest consists of dry seaweed, grasses and flotsam. Two or three light-brown, dark blotched eggs are laid from August to December. Both sexes incubate for three and a half weeks. The cryptically coloured (camouflaged) chicks remain in or near the nest for several days and can fly when five weeks old.

# Black-billed gull *Larus bulleri* 37 cm

*Black-billed gull, chicks in crèche.*

The endemic black-billed gull is mainly an inland bird, frequenting South Island riverbeds and lakes. Some birds are found on rivers in Hawke's Bay and a few inhabit, as well as nest, in coastal regions of the Manukau Harbour, Firth of Thames and eastern Bay of Plenty in the North Island. In winter months, many birds move to coastal areas to feed. Black-billed gulls are not confiding with humans and will only rarely make a close approach for scraps of food. They are also slimmer in build than the red-billed gull, with a noticeably narrower bill. With immature birds, buff tips edge the feathers of the mantle and back. In inland areas the birds' food consists of insects and their larvae and earthworms. In the South Island they can often be seen following the plough. On the coast, small fish, crustaceans and molluscs form their diet. Most black-billed gulls nest in colonies on several shingle riverbeds in the South Island and sometimes on the shores of lakes. In the North Island a thriving colony has nested for many years on the shores of Lake Rotorua, and are joined by nesting red-billed gulls. In recent years several small colonies of black-billed gulls have nested successfully on some North Island sheltered coasts, notably at Miranda in the Firth of Thames, the Manukau Harbour and Ohope. Nests are composed of sticks, grasses and twigs. In coastal colonies dried seaweed is also added. Two buff-coloured, darkly marked eggs are laid from October to December, with both sexes incubating for about 25 days. When the chicks are about 10 days old, they congregate in crèches, which a few parents take turns at guarding.

**Black-fronted tern** *Sterna albostriata* 30 cm

The endemic black-fronted tern is mainly a South Island bird, frequenting rivers and farmlands on the eastern side of the Southern Alps. In winter, many birds migrate to coastal estuaries, some in the North Island. They are easily distinguished from the common white-fronted tern by their smaller size and bright orange bill and feet. After nesting, the black head cap becomes mottled after moulting. Black-fronted terns are dainty feeders. They fly above the surface of rivers to snatch insects, and occasionally plunge to seize small fish. Over farmland, they hawk insects and land to search for earthworms and grass grubs. In winter months they feed on marine crustaceans and plankton. Black-fronted terns nest in loose colonies on shingle banks on many South Island rivers, sometimes associating with nesting black-billed gulls. The nest is a scrape in patches of sand between river stones, and sparsely lined with a few sticks or grasses. Egg colour varies from grey to brown, darkly blotched. The usual clutch of two or three eggs is laid from late September to November. Incubation, which takes just over three weeks, is shared by the sexes. Chicks remain in or around the nest for the first few days and are able to fly when four and a half weeks old.

## Caspian tern *Sterna caspia* 51 cm

The Caspian tern, an almost cosmopolitan species, is the world's largest tern. It is easily recognised by its large size and bright red bill. In flight, the shortish tail and sickle-shaped wings distinguish it from the other terns seen in New Zealand. Caspian terns are seen throughout New Zealand, mainly feeding close to the shore and exploring the length of tidal estuaries. They are also seen inland on lakes and rivers, usually alone or in twos or threes. Like other terns, Caspian terns feed only on live fish, which are captured after a clumsy dive. In marine habitats they catch small mullet, flounders and piper. In freshwater habitats the birds take carp, trout and sometimes small eels. Some Caspian terns nest as isolated pairs on small offshore islets, shellspits, on shores of inland lakes and even on small beaches within city harbours and estuaries. Nests are a scrape in the sand or shells, and separated about 1 or 2 metres from neighbours. They lay two or three surprisingly large eggs that are buff-coloured and darkly spotted. Both sexes take turns at incubation, which lasts for three weeks. Chicks remain in the nest for five or six days and are fed with whole fish, sometimes too large for the chick to swallow, especially when sand adheres to the food. Chicks can fly when five weeks old.

**White-fronted tern** *Sterna striata* 42 cm

The white-fronted tern is the most common tern, being found throughout New Zealand. They are most frequently seen on the east coasts of the North and South Islands, but in winter months large flocks inhabit west coast beaches. Also in winter months, young birds and some adults migrate to the east coast of Australia, but do not breed there. White-fronted terns feed by scanning the sea surface and diving with a splash to capture small fish, often feeding close to the shore. At other times, flocks of the birds dive for small fish chased to the surface by predatory kahawai fish. In these situations they are often accompanied by red-billed gulls, shearwaters and even gannets. In colonies on shellbanks, sand dunes, rock islets and at Kaikoura, white-fronted terns nest in association with red-billed gulls. The nest is a scrape in the ground, without added nesting material. One or two eggs are laid from October to January. Adults share incubation of the buff-coloured, darkly marked eggs. Incubation takes three and a half weeks. Chicks, which are covered in peppery-coloured down, remain in the nest for about four days. Later they join a crèche that is protected by different parents in turn. Chicks are able to fly when five weeks old, but continue to be fed by their parents.

**Fairy tern** *Sterna nereis* 25 cm

The fairy tern is New Zealand's smallest and rarest breeding tern, now found only on the east coast of Northland and the Kaipara Harbour. Little is known of their movements after nesting. However, groups in eclipse plumage roost with the similar-sized eastern little tern (see below), on sandspits in the inner Kaipara Harbour. Fairy terns feed by hovering and then diving to capture small fish, such as anchovies, sprats and small flounder, mostly on tidal river estuaries. In October, nest scrapes are made in an area of broken shell. The usual clutch consists of two pale-grey, lightly brown-spotted eggs and incubation is shared by the sexes over 24 days. Chicks are brooded in the nest for two days then, their cryptic colouration matching the sand, they wander off, hiding under driftwood. Chicks are able to fly when 21 days old.

**Eastern little tern** *Sterna albifrons* 25 cm

A few of these small terns, which do not nest in New Zealand, spend the summer months on northern harbours here, some migrating as far as Stewart Island. Their feeding habits are similar to those of the fairy tern. They can usually be distinguished by the black tip to their yellow bill and the black cap reaching to the base of the bill. Birds in breeding plumage show black edges to their primary wing feathers, but in eclipse plumage they are difficult to differentiate from immature fairy terns.

### New Zealand pigeon *Hemiphaga novaeseelandiae* 51 cm

The New Zealand pigeon is New Zealand's only endemic species of pigeon. It is widely distributed in forest habitats throughout the country and offshore islands. It is also seen in some open country areas where there are trees, as the birds are attracted to feed on the flowers of broom and white clover. The pigeon is easily approached, and identified by its large size, general greyish-green colour and pure white breast. In flight, the birds' heavy wingbeats produce a low, whistling sound. New Zealand pigeons are of prime ecological importance, as by feeding on the fruits of many native trees and shrubs, they disperse the seeds over a wide area, in their droppings. They are strictly vegetarian, feeding on succulent shoots, flowers and the fruits of many tree species. They are the only bird able to swallow the large fruits of karaka and puriri. The nests of New Zealand pigeons can be found during many months of the year, with egg laying probably dependent on food availability. Generally, most birds nest between August and January. The nest is usually a flimsy structure of sticks, in which a single, small white egg is laid. Both sexes share incubation for four weeks and the chick is first fed by regurgitating pigeon milk, a protein-rich secretion from the parent's crop. This is gradually supplemented by fruit pulp with the chick being finally fed on regurgitated whole fruits. The chick usually fledges when about six weeks old. In some cases, when food is plentiful, a second nest is commenced before the first chick has fledged.

### Barbary dove *Streptopelia roseogrisea* 28 cm

The small number of barbary doves in the wild originated from escaped cage birds. The population is scattered widely in the North Island, inhabiting open country where there are trees, and urban parks. They feed mainly on seeds, fruits, succulent buds and clover as well as on grain in stubble fields. The birds also sometimes feed on seeds from dry sludge piles near sewage works. Barbary doves rear several broods in a season. They build a nest of small sticks in hedges or in forks of trees. Two white eggs form the normal clutch, which are incubated for two weeks by both parents. Chicks are fed on regurgitated crop milk, later supplemented with fruit and seeds. Chicks fledge when just over two weeks of age.

### Spotted dove *Streptopelia chinensis* 30 cm

Spotted doves were introduced to New Zealand from various Asian countries. They are reasonably common in open country with sheltering trees, in south Auckland and Auckland city parks. They also inhabit orchards and open country in the eastern Bay of Plenty. The birds feed mainly on grass seeds and clover and sometimes eat spilt grain in horse paddocks, and invertebrates. Spotted doves make a call with a repeated 'cruu-cruu' sound, very similar to that of the barbary dove. The two birds are distinguished by the spotted dove's lack of a prominent black neck collar. The birds raise several broods in a season. They lay two white eggs in a flimsy nest of twigs built in a shrub or tree fork. Both sexes incubate for 16 days, feeding the chicks by regurgitating crop milk and fruit. Chicks fledge when 16 days old.

COLUMBIDAE

The common rock pigeon is found throughout New Zealand. Birds inhabiting towns and cities are sedentary and do not fly long distances to find food. However, feral rock pigeons inhabit rural areas, particularly in districts where crops are grown, such as Canterbury and Hawke's Bay. In some locations they roost and nest on cliff ledges, flying some distance to feed on riverbeds and agricultural land. In urban environments rock pigeons feed on seeds in parklands and a wide variety of food scraps provided by humans. In rural areas their main food consists of seed from grasses and weeds. They may cause damage to crops, especially newly sown corn and peas. Rock pigeons breed throughout many months of the year, building a flimsy nest of twigs and grasses on the ledge of a building or cliff and sometimes in caves. The usual clutch of two white eggs is incubated by both sexes for 18 days. Chicks fledge when 30 days old.

### Sulphur-crested cockatoo *Cacatua galerita* 50 cm

New Zealand's population of sulphur-crested cockatoos is thought to have originated from escaped cage birds. But there is also the possibility that some birds are self-introduced from Australia. They are found in scattered groups throughout the North Island and in Canterbury. The largest populations are in the western Waikato and in the Turakina River catchment, west of Taihape. Sulphur-crested cockatoos feed on grasses and thistle seeds, fruits of weeds, shrubs and podocarp trees, and also dig insect grubs from rotten tree branches. After nesting, they form large flocks and are extremely wary, and so are difficult to approach. The birds nest in holes and cavities in large trees, laying two or three white eggs, which are incubated by both sexes.

### Kakapo *Strigops habroptilus* 63 cm

The highly endangered endemic kakapo is the world's largest and most distinctive parrot, being flightless, nocturnal in habit and indulging in a 'lek' courtship display. This feature of courtship behaviour is usually performed by some species of grouse. Kakapo were reasonably common in Fiordland in the early 1900s, but with the arrival of stoats in the area, their numbers plummeted rapidly. Remaining birds from Fiordland and Stewart Island have now been relocated on predator-free Codfish Island off the north-west coast of Stewart Island. A few are kept and monitored on Maud Island in the Marlborough Sounds. The total population of kakapo was 86 birds in 2006. Kakapo feed on the seeds of many plants, particularly tussock and flax seeds, and fallen fruits of podocarp and rimu trees, and leaves of succulent plants. They also grub for roots. The birds are irregular in nesting habits, and it appears they only breed in the years when abundant fruits are available, particularly those of the rimu tree. With 'lek' breeding, the male constructs an arena, or display area, and calls to the females to be mated. The male kakapo's arena consists of a series of scraped bowls in the ground, connected by tracks trimmed of vegetation. These arenas, situated on high ground, are occupied by the male at night. From here, with a repeatedly low booming call, he signals to attract the female to mate. Females alone prepare a shallow burrow and lay two or three white eggs that she incubates for four weeks. Chicks fledge when about 12 weeks old and remain with, and are fed by, the female.

# Kaka *Nestor meridionalis* 45 cm

The kaka inhabits the larger tracts of native forest on the mainland and on forested offshore islands. The South Island populations are located in Westland, Fiordland and Stewart Island, but the bird is uncommon east of the Southern Alps. Being strong fliers, some birds migrate from offshore islands to mainland habitats in winter months, and may even be seen feeding in suburban gardens. Kaka numbers have been reduced by stoat predation, with females often killed on the nest while incubating. And as chicks remain on or near the ground for the first three days after fledging, they are vulnerable to predation. In the Nelson Lakes National Park, effective stoat control has resulted in a marked increase in the number of surviving kaka chicks. The birds feed on succulent shoots and fruits of a variety of plants. With their spatulate tongues they drink nectar from pohutukawa and rata, as well as the honeydew from the trunks of beech trees. With their powerful bill they rip off bark and rotten wood to take insect larvae such as huhu grubs. Kaka are specific in their nesting requirements, choosing dry cavities in large trees to lay three or four white eggs on a bed of fine wood chips. Nesting extends from September to February, and the female alone incubates the clutch for about 24 days. The male calls her from the nest approximately every 80 minutes to feed her on regurgitated vegetable matter, each feed lasting three or four minutes. Chicks fledge when nine or 10 weeks old but are almost flightless for the first few days, and stay with their parents for at least six months.

**Kea** *Nestor notabilis* 46 cm

The endemic kea is the world's only alpine parrot, inhabiting high altitude forests and the alpine herbfields of the South Island. They also descend to valleys and lowland areas, sometimes invading rubbish tips of high-country settlements. Kea are inquisitive and playful, often doing damage to vehicles in skifield carparks, such as removing windscreen wipers. Their playful antics sometimes disturb inhabitants of alpine ski huts. Kea are strong fliers and are often seen tumbling in turbulent mountain air currents (updraughts), displaying their bright orange-coloured under-wings. The birds feed mainly on alpine vegetation, particularly fruits of shrubs and snowberries. Some rogue birds attack sick sheep, usually at night, tearing the flesh from the sheep's back. Unlike other parrots, kea use lichens, twigs and grasses to line their nests. They are usually situated in clefts of tumbled rocks, or in a shallow burrow under tree roots. Two or four white eggs are laid between August and December, being incubated for three and a half weeks by the female. She is fed by the male, who also feeds the chicks when they are older. Chicks leave the nest when about 14 weeks old. Immature kea can be recognised by their yellow-coloured cere and eye ring.

## Galah *Cacatua roseicapilla* 36 cm

A small population of this Australian cockatoo inhabits areas of forest and open country near the Hunua Ranges in South Auckland and in lower Waikato River regions. The New Zealand population originated from escaped cage birds. They feed on a variety of seeds and shoots of shrubs. Their nesting habits have not been studied in New Zealand, but in Australia the birds nest in cavities of trees.

## Eastern rosella *Platycerus eximius* 32 cm

The colourful rosella parakeet, an Australian species, is common in many parts of the North Island, particularly Northland. There is also a small population in south Otago. These populations originated from escaped cage birds. They inhabit forests, open country with tree shelter, and orchards. They feed on shoots of shrubs, thistle seeds and fruits of many trees, especially podocarps. They also take insects, particularly when nesting. Eastern rosellas begin nesting in October, choosing a dry tree cavity, a hollow in the end of a broken tree limb or, in particular, a cavity in the trunk of a dead tree fern. The usual clutch of four to eight white eggs is incubated by the female for just over three weeks. Chicks fledge when four weeks old.

The endemic yellow-crowned parakeet is widespread in the South Island. The bird is less common in the North Island but may be found in podocarp forests and higher altitude beech forest of the central North Island and the Tararua Range. They are more common on many offshore islands where they are safe from predation. Yellow-crowned parakeets feed on shoots of shrubs, fruits, flower buds, seeds of beech trees, and, unlike the red-crowned parakeet, frequently feeds on insects, particularly aphid and scale insects. They are often difficult to observe as they usually feed in the forest canopy, and infrequently feed on, or near the ground. The birds nest in holes of large trees or in cavities formed in the end of broken tree limbs. Four to eight eggs are laid from October to January and incubated by the female for three weeks. Chicks fledge when five weeks old.

# Red-crowned parakeet *Cyanoramphus novaezelandiae* 28 cm

The red-crowned parakeet is becoming increasingly rare on the mainland, due to the fact that they often feed on the ground and are subject to predation by feral cats and stoats. They still occur in heavily forested areas of the North Island, but apart from populations in north-west Nelson, they are rare in the South Island. Thriving populations exist on Stewart Island and many offshore islands, where they are often seen feeding on seeds and flax. Their main diet consists of the seeds of flax, tussock and grasses, fruits of podocarp and various shrubs, nectar and flower buds. They do not feed as frequently on invertebrates as the yellow-eyed parakeet. Red-crowned parakeets choose holes in hollow trees or cavities where large branches have broken from large trees. Eggs are laid between October and January, with the clutch of up to nine white eggs being incubated for three weeks by the female. While incubating, the male calls the female from the nest to feed her with regurgitated vegetable matter. This process often lasts for five minutes. When the chicks are large, the female frequently leaves the nest. In these instances the male will enter the nest and feed them. Chicks fledge at between six and seven weeks.

### Long-tailed cuckoo *Eudynamys taitensis* 40 cm

The endemic long-tailed cuckoo has a very hawk-like appearance, with its brown streaked plumage and slightly hooked bill. In flight they are unmistakable, as the tail is slightly longer than the head and body. After wintering in the forests of islands in the Bismarck Archipelago and the Solomon Islands, they begin arriving in northern New Zealand in October, then gradually move south. Some stay in the North Island habitats occupied by whiteheads, while others go to the South and Stewart Islands, where they parasitise brown creepers and yellowheads. Food includes insects, spiders and lizards. They also rob eggs from other birds' nests. The female

*Long-tailed cuckoo, captive.*

lays a single egg in several nests: of the whitehead in the North Island and of the brown creeper and yellowhead in the South Island. The cuckoo then leaves the foster parent to hatch the egg and feed the chick. Adults return to the tropics in March and April, with the chicks following later.

### Shining cuckoo *Chrysococcyx lucidus* 16 cm

This small cuckoo arrives in New Zealand in September, announcing its presence with its repeated whistle of rising notes and then a descending inflection. They are common in suburban gardens and forests throughout New Zealand. The birds prey on caterpillars, insects and spiders. In late October and November the female lays a single egg in the domed nest of a grey warbler. The young cuckoo, when hatched, soon evicts any grey warbler chick or egg remaining in the nest. It is then reared by the foster parents and continues to be fed for several weeks after fledging. The diminutive grey warbler is only a quarter of the size of its foster chick. Shining cuckoos return to winter in the tropical islands in and adjacent to the Solomon Islands.

**Morepork** *Ninox novaeseelandiae* 29 cm

The morepork is New Zealand's only native owl. The larger laughing owl became extinct in the early 20th century. Moreporks are widely distributed throughout forested areas of North, South and Stewart Islands and most forested offshore islands. They are uncommon in open country regions of the eastern South Island. Some have adapted to live in open country where there are clumps of trees. They are also seen in parks and suburban built-up areas where they hawk moths attracted to street lamps. Moreporks feed mainly on large insects, especially moths and weta. They also take mice, small birds and nocturnal geckos. The birds nest in holes in trees, in cavities under clumps of perching epiphytes and sometimes in the fork of a large pine tree. The normal clutch laid in October or November is two or occasionally three, almost round, white eggs. Incubation is performed by the female, with the male feeding her at the nest or calling her to receive food. Chicks hatch after 30 or 31 days, blind and covered in grey down. The male starts hunting at dusk and bringing the first food, which is a mouse or small bird, to the nest. The female feeds herself, then tears pieces for the chicks. After this first large feed, most food items consist of insects. Chicks leave the nest at four and a half weeks old and then remain with the parents for at least three weeks.

**Little owl** *Athene noctua* 23 cm

Little owls were introduced to New Zealand from Germany in the early 1900s to prey on sparrows, which were damaging crops in the South Island. They are absent from the North Island and Stewart Island. Here they are seldom seen in forested areas, but are most commonly seen in drier eastern regions. The birds are easily distinguished from the morepork. They have a less rounded head, shorter tail and their plumage is lighter in colour. These owls are frequently seen in daylight, perched on fence posts or trees. Their main diet consists of insects, spiders and earthworms, often caught by the owl as it walks and searches the ground. They also catch small birds and mice. Little owls begin nesting in October, choosing a hole in a tree, an old rabbit burrow or nesting in stacks of baled hay. The clutch of two to four white eggs is incubated by the female for 28 days. The male brings her food at the nest. When about two weeks old, like morepork chicks, they emerge from the nest at night to await food brought by each parent. Chicks remain with the parents for a few weeks after fledging.

# Kingfisher *Halcyon sancta* 24 cm

The kingfisher is common throughout mainland New Zealand, Stewart Island and many offshore islands. They inhabit a wide variety of habitats extending over sheltered coasts and harbours, open farmlands, wetlands, lake shores and inland rivers as well as in the depths of some forests. They are most common in northern coastal areas, as in winter months, when insects become scarce inland, most birds migrate to the coast. Kingfishers are wary birds. They are frequently seen perched on powerlines, trees and posts, waiting to dive to capture insects, earthworms or in coastal districts they perch on rocks on the lookout for mudcrabs or small fish in rockpools. Prey, such as lizards, larger fish, or mice, are bashed on hard surfaces to make it supple before being swallowed whole. In summer, kingfishers take large numbers of cicadas and crickets. The birds begin selecting a nest site in September, boring a tunnel in a rotten tree or clay bank and often among the roots of a fallen tree. A clutch of up to six eggs is laid in October or November. Incubation is mainly by the female, with the male taking short spells of two or three hours. Chicks hatch after 21 days and are fed by each parent, on whole insects, fish and even whole mice, which are swallowed head-first. Chicks fledge when 26 days old, remaining with the parents for several days.

**Kookaburra** *Dacelo novaeguineae* 45 cm

Kookaburras were introduced to Kawau Island, in the Hauraki
Gulf, from Australia in the 1860s. They bred and extended their
range to the adjacent mainland, now inhabiting rural land from
Wellsford in the north to as far south as the northern Waitakere
Ranges. Due, possibly, to a lack of such large food items as snakes
and lizards, breeding is often unsuccessful, with chicks often dying
before reaching maturity. Kookaburra feed on large insects, earthworms, lizards, small birds and rodents. In true kingfisher fashion,
they sit on a prominent post or tree branch and dive to catch their
prey. The 'catch' is swallowed whole and head-first. The birds nest
in cavities in large pohutukawa trees and sometimes bore nesting
tunnels in dead trees. Two or three white eggs are laid from
November to January and incubation takes 24 days. Chicks fledge
when five weeks old.

**Welcome swallow** *Hirundo tahitica* 15 cm

This Australian species introduced itself to Northland in the late 1950s and successful nests were seen under road and river bridges in 1957. They soon spread throughout the North and South Islands. Welcome swallows inhabit open country, swamps, rivers and the coast. With a swift, circling flight the birds hawk insects, particularly over water, catching the insects in the air. After a spell of flying, they settle, perching on fences, raupo stems and bare branches of trees. In winter months, when insect food becomes scarce inland, many welcome swallows migrate to beaches and feed on kelp flies. Welcome swallows build a nest composed of mud reinforced with grasses and lined with feathers. This is attached to concrete walls under bridges, ledges in farm buildings and in caves. Three to five pale pink eggs are laid from August to February.

### Rifleman *Acanthisitta chloris* 8 cm

The endemic rifleman is New Zealand's smallest bird. They inhabit native and exotic forests throughout the country and some forested offshore islands. Apart from small populations in Coromandel and a kauri forest in Northland, they are absent north of Waikato. The birds are mostly seen in high-altitude beech forests in the central North Island and are common in South Island beech forests. Riflemen feed on insects and their larvae, spiders and occasionally small fruits. They obtain most of their food by delving into the bark of trees and searching lichens and mosses. The birds begin nesting in September, rearing more than one brood in a season. The nest is a globe of fine grasses and moss, lined with feathers and built under a piece of flaking bark, in a knothole of a tree trunk, or sometimes in a hole of a bank. Both sexes incubate the clutch of three or four eggs, for three weeks. The parents are often assisted in feeding the chicks by the young from a previous brood.

### Rock wren *Xenicus gilviventris* 9 cm

The endemic rock wren is found only in the South Island, where it inhabits alpine herbfields especially in areas where tumbled rocks are interspersed with alpine shrubs. Rock wrens are only slightly larger than riflemen, but can be recognised by their longer legs, large feet and a habit of bobbing up and down. Like riflemen, they are weak fliers. Their food consists of insects and their larvae, and spiders. In winter when snow covers the herbfields, it is thought that rock wrens live and feed in the cavities of piles of fallen rocks. Rock wrens build a globe-shaped nest of grasses lined with feathers, in a rock crevice. Two or three white eggs are incubated by both sexes for three weeks.

**New Zealand pipit** *Anthus novaeseelandiae* 19 cm

The New Zealand pipit is widely distributed throughout the country. It inhabits rough pastures, riverbeds, sandy beaches and forest margins. It is also found at high altitudes. Although of similar colour, it can be distinguished from the introduced skylark by its slimmer build and a habit of persistent tail flicking. It does not soar high in the sky as does the skylark. Pipits eat a wide range of insects and their larvae. On beaches they also take sandhoppers and kelp flies. As well, the birds eat grass seeds and clover. New Zealand pipits nest from September to February, building a loose nest of grasses in rough herbage, usually on a bank or on the ground under bracken. The female incubates the clutch of three or four eggs for 15 days. Both parents feed the chicks, which fledge when 15 days old. The population of pipits in many arable areas has been severely reduced with predation of nests by introduced Australian magpies.

## Skylark *Alauda arvensis* 18 cm

Skylarks were introduced to New Zealand from Europe in the 1860s. They are common throughout New Zealand and many off-shore islands. Skylarks prefer pastures and arable land, but also inhabit sand dunes and subalpine herbfields. The birds are noted for their vibrant, rippling song, performed by the male bird as he soars up to 100 metres in the air. They sometimes sing when perched on a fence post. Unlike pipits, skylarks feed mainly on seeds of a variety of plants. However, they take insects and grubs when feeding their chicks. Skylarks rear two or three broods a year, building a nest of fine grasses in a depression in the ground, often in very short pastures. The three to five grey, speckled eggs are incubated by the female for 11 days. The chicks fledge when 12 days old. In some districts skylarks have been eliminated due to predation by Australian magpies, who rob nests of eggs or chicks. This predation has been recorded on film, where a magpie was seen feeding in a grass paddock. It flew to its nest and fed one of its chicks with a fledgling bird. The only ground-nesting birds in this area were skylarks.

## Blackbird *Turdus merula* 25 cm

*Blackbird, female with chicks (top).*

Blackbirds were introduced to New Zealand from Europe in the 1860s. They are common throughout the mainland and many off-shore islands. They inhabit urban gardens and parks as well as arable and pastoral regions where there are trees and hedges. They are sometimes found in alpine herbfields and even in the depths of the forests, where they are extremely wary. The birds feed on a wide variety of foods. Blackbirds are frequently seen pecking for earthworms and other invertebrates and their larvae. They eat fruits from many shrubs as well as podocarp trees and nikau palms. They cause considerable damage in commercial orchards. Male blackbirds sing more melodiously than any of the introduced passerines. But the birds do not begin to sing until early spring, unlike the song thrush, which often begins singing in late autumn. Blackbirds rear several broods during the year, from July to January. The nest, built in hedges or forks of trees, is composed of twigs, leaves and grasses and reinforced with mud. The eggs are bluish-green, marked with brown blotches and are incubated by the female for 13 days. The male assists in feeding the chicks, which fledge when 14 days old.

**Song thrush** *Turdus philomelos* 23 cm

The song thrush was introduced from Europe in the 1860s at the same time as the blackbird. It is common in suburban gardens, parks, scrub and exotic forest. Unlike the blackbird, it does not venture to the depths of native forest, although some birds are seen in subalpine habitats. The bird feeds on a range of insects and their larvae, earthworms and spiders. They are particularly fond of garden snails, which they bash on a favoured rock or pathway. Song thrushes begin their song in autumn or early winter, with three-syllable repeated notes. They begin nesting as early as May in northern districts. The nest, built in dense shrubs or forks of trees, is composed of twigs and grasses and lined with mud. Four or five sky-blue, black-spotted eggs are incubated by the female for 13 days. The chicks are fed by both parents and fledge when 14 days old.

# Hedge sparrow (Dunnock) *Prunella modularis* 14 cm

The hedge sparrow was another species introduced to New Zealand from Europe in the 1860s and is now found throughout the country. They were rare north of Auckland until the mid-1900s. Hedge sparrows are very secretive and are usually seen on the ground under the cover of hedges and shrubs. They inhabit suburban gardens, parks and open country where there is a shelter of shrubbery. The birds are insectivorous, feeding on insects and their larvae, spiders and small earthworms. They build a very neat nest placed in dense hedges or gorse bush and composed of small twigs, grasses and moss. The clutch of four or five sky-blue eggs is incubated by the female for 12 days. The male assists in feeding the chicks, which fledge when 14 days old. Hedge sparrows often inhabit high-altitude alpine herbfields, where they have been recorded nesting in stunted shrubs.

## Whitehead *Mohoua albicilla* 15 cm

The endemic whitehead is found only in the North Island and some of its offshore islands. Apart from Little Barrier and Tiritiri Matangi Islands, they are absent from Northland. They are common in native and exotic forests and scrub south of the Waikato, also inhabiting exotic pine forest with fragments of native shrubs. Whiteheads are active feeders, digging into the bark of trees and hanging from branches to search for caterpillars, spiders and other insects. They also eat fruits from native shrubs and some podocarp trees. The birds are usually found feeding in family groups, but they pair off to nest from October to January with two females often accompanying the male. A neat nest of grasses, moss and treefern fronds is built in a shrub or fork of a tree. The female incubates the clutch of three or four eggs for 17 days. Chicks are fed by both parents, assisted by a second female and, sometimes, immature birds. Chicks fledge when 17 days old. Whiteheads are one of the species used as foster parents for long-tailed cuckoo eggs and chicks.

## Yellowhead *Mohoua ochrocephala* 15 cm

The endemic yellowhead is found only in the South Island. Its numbers have declined in recent years due mainly to predation by stoats. The main populations of yellowheads are located in the beech forests of Eglinton Valley, Fiordland and Mount Aspiring National Park. Small populations survive in the Catlins as well as isolated groups in parts of the Marlborough Sounds. Yellowheads have similar feeding habits to whiteheads, taking insects and spiders from tree trunks and foliage. They also eat small fruits. The birds also build a nest similar in construction to that of the whitehead. However, instead of being built in a shrub, the yellowhead's nest is built in a hole or cavity in a large, often rotting tree. The female incubates the clutch of two or three eggs for 20 days. At this time the bird is vulnerable to predation by stoats. This has resulted in a disproportionate number of males to females.

### Brown creeper *Mohoua novaeseelandiae* 13 cm

The endemic brown creeper is found only in the South Island, Stewart Island and on some of its offshore islands. The birds inhabit native and exotic forests, manuka scrub, and are located up to the treeline in alpine territories. They are active feeders, eating a wide variety of insects and their larvae and spiders, often by hanging upside down to pluck insects from beneath leaves. The birds also eat small fruits. Brown creepers nest from September to January, and are double brooded. Their nests, built in thick shrubbery, are composed of grasses, lichen and moss, bound with cobwebs and lined with feathers. The female incubates the clutch of two or three eggs for 19 days, with both parents feeding the chicks, which fledge when 20 days old. The second nest is often chosen by the long-tailed cuckoo to lay its egg, to be hatched and reared by the brown creeper. The cuckoo chick when fledged is considerably larger than its foster parent.

**Grey warbler** *Gerygone igata* 11 cm

The endemic grey warbler inhabits native and exotic forests, scrubland and suburban gardens throughout New Zealand and offshore islands. They feed on a variety of insects and their larvae and spiders. They sometimes hover in the air to pick insects from leaves on the outer branches of shrubs. The grey warbler is the only New Zealand bird to build a hanging nest. The intricate, domed nest is often hanging from a tree's outer branches with the point of suspension firmly woven around a branch. The lower part is sometimes secured at one side to prevent it swinging. Grasses, lichen, moss, wool and spider web are used to construct the nest, leaving just a small entrance hole on one side. Clutches of three or four eggs are laid from August to December. The female incubates for 19 days and the chicks fledge when 18 days old. The later brood is often parasitised by the migrant shining cuckoo.

## Fantail *Rhipidura fuliginosa* 16 cm

The fantail inhabits native and exotic forests, manuka scrub and suburban gardens throughout New Zealand as well as offshore islands. In northern regions most fantails are brown and light plumaged, but it is common to see fantails in a black plumage phase in the South Island. Fantails feed on a variety of insects, grubs and spiders. Many flying insects such as moths and flies are caught on the wing, by hawking. The presumed friendliness of fantails, when making a close approach to humans, is due to people disturbing insects from foliage. In winter months some fantails flock together to catch insects disturbed on farm pastures. In seasons of plentiful food, fantails occasionally raise four or five broods. Nesting extends from early August to March. Most nests are placed on a single stem of a shrub branch or treefern frond, frequently overhanging a stream. The female builds a compact nest composed of fine grasses, lichen, moss and small pieces of bark, which she binds tightly with cobweb, and it is completed in only three days. The nest is usually left with an untidy tail hanging below. Two or three cream-coloured, brown-spotted eggs are incubated by both sexes for 15 days. After 14 days the chicks bulge from the small nest and usually then leave it, perching together on a nearby branch, where they are fed frequently by both parents.

119

**Tomtit** *Petroica macrocephala* 13 cm

*Tomtit: male (top); female (bottom).*

Two subspecies of the endemic tomtit inhabit mainland New Zealand, Stewart Island and offshore islands. The North Island tomtit is black with a white breast. Females are brownish with a whitish wing bar, and in the South Island males show a yellow-tinged breast. Tomtits inhabit native and exotic forests, and tall manuka and kanuka; they are especially common in some beech forests. The birds feed on insects and their larvae and earthworms. When observed in forests it is usual to see only the male birds, who seem inquisitive of intruders. In autumn months tomtits also feed on small fruits. Nesting extends from August to January. The female builds a bulky nest composed of grasses, lichen, moss and treefern fronds bound together with cobwebs. The nests are usually well camouflaged and often difficult to find. They are built in the forks of trees, in shallow cavities of rotting tree trunks or in the ends of broken branches. Nests may also be built on the sides of treefern trunks. Three or four cream-coloured, brown-marked eggs form the usual clutch, incubated by the female for 17 days. Chicks are fed by both parents and fledge when 18 days old. Chicks are attended by the male bird only when the female builds a later nest and incubates a second clutch.

# New Zealand robin *Petroica australis* 18 cm

New Zealand robins inhabit mature native forests and some exotic forests throughout the country. The North Island subspecies is absent north of Auckland, apart from recent introductions to the Wenderholm Reserve and Tiritiri Matangi Island, but are widespread in other native forests. The South Island subspecies is common apart from in eastern regions. The Stewart Island subspecies is well established. Due to the robin's habit of regularly feeding on the forest floor, they are subject to predation by stoats and feral cats, and nests are also often predated by rats. Robins feed on a variety of insects and their larvae, and spiders. They will take large insects, such as weta and stick insects. They also eat earthworms. In forests, robins will make a close approach to humans in their search for invertebrates disturbed by trampers' feet. Robins raise three broods in a season, from August to January. The nest is a bulky structure composed of twigs, dry grasses, lichens and moss, usually lined with fine grasses and a few feathers. It is built in the fork of a tree or large shrub or in the shallow crevice of a large tree. Two or three cream-coloured, brown-marked eggs are incubated by the female for 18 days, with the chicks fledging when three weeks old.

The **black robin**, ***Petroica traversi***, which was miraculously saved from extinction, is found only on Mangere and Southeast Islands in the Chathams.

**Silvereye** *Zosterops lateralis* 12 cm

The silvereye introduced itself from Australia in 1856. It is now widespread and very common throughout New Zealand. It inhabits native and exotic forests, scrub, orchards as well as suburban gardens where they visit garden bird tables to eat scraps, fat and sugar water. In northern districts they take insects from stands of mangroves. After the breeding season, silvereyes form groups and move through gardens eating aphids, caterpillars and scale insects. With their brush tongues they drink nectar from many flowering plants, but cause damage to ripe fruit and, often, considerable damage to orchard fruits and grapes in vineyards. Silvereyes eat a wide variety of insects and their larvae, and spiders, sometimes capturing large insects such as cicadas and katydids. They eat and disperse seeds from fruit of podocarp trees, particularly kahikatea, and are responsible for spreading weed seeds, such as inkweed. The birds raise two or three broods in a year, nesting from August to February. The nest, composed of fine grasses, lichens and moss, is built in hedges, the outermost branches of trees, notably pines and macrocarpa and also stands of bamboo. Both sexes incubate the three or four pale-blue eggs for 11 days and chicks fledge when 11 or 12 days old. They remain as a family group until the next nest is constructed.

### Fernbird *Bowdleria punctata* 18 cm

There are four species of the endemic fernbird widely distributed throughout New Zealand and some offshore islands. A fifth species is found on the Snares Islands, south of Stewart Island. Fernbirds are very weak fliers, and are unique in that the barbs of their tails are disconnected, giving the tails a fern-like appearance. The birds are uncommon in the drier regions east of the Southern Alps, occurring more frequently in many wetlands, in sedge-blanketed saltmarshes and in some areas of flax and scrub. But as the birds are secretive, remaining within the cover of vegetation, they are infrequently seen, although they can often be persuaded to show themselves, by calling with a high-pitched double whistle. Fernbirds feed on insects and their larvae, and spiders. In swamplands they often conveniently find nurseryweb spiders. Fernbirds have an extended nesting season, with eggs laid from August to March. The nest is a loose structure composed of dried grasses and lined with feathers. It is built a few centimetres above ground in rushes, cutty grass or sedges. Sometimes nests built among the sedges of saltmarshes are inundated by high spring tides. The three or four pink, purple-spotted eggs are incubated by both parents for 14 days. The chicks fledge when 16 days old.

**Stitchbird** *Notiomystis cincta* 18 cm

*Stitchbird: male (top); female (bottom).*

The endemic endangered stitchbird is found only in the North Island, where the species was widespread in several forests until the late 1800s. However, predation by rats and mustelids and possibly an introduced avian disease eliminated stitchbirds from the mainland. They survived only on Little Barrier Island in the Hauraki Gulf, where their numbers were kept low as a result of predation by feral cats. Following the extermination of cats on the island, stitchbird numbers have increased. This has allowed the Department of Conservation to transfer several birds to other predator-free offshore islands. As some of the transferred birds have met competition for food from the larger, more aggressive bellbird and tui, supplementary feeding has been provided in feeders that exclude the larger birds. Stitchbirds feed on nectar and fruits from various native trees and shrubs. They also take invertebrates, especially when feeding chicks. The stitchbird nests in holes of trees. Nests, which are constructed above the nest hole entrance, are composed of sticks, grasses and treefern scales, and are given a soft lining of feathers. Two or three broods are raised in a season, with the clutch of three or four eggs incubated by the female for 15 days. The chicks are fed by both parents and fledge when four weeks old.

### Bellbird *Anthornis melanura* 20 cm

*Bellbird: male (top); female (right).*

The endemic bellbird is widely distributed throughout New Zealand and offshore islands. However, apart from thriving populations on the Northland offshore islands, it is absent north of Auckland. The previous population in this region died out in the late 1800s probably due to a combination of predation and introduced avian disease. Bellbirds on offshore islands and the rest of New Zealand, although threatened by predators, apparently did not contact the disease. Bellbirds are particularly noted for their melodious song, being one of the few species to sing during most months of the year. The birds inhabit native and exotic forests, scrublands, some city parks and suburban gardens. With their brush tongue they sip nectar from many native and exotic flowering plants, particularly kowhai, pohutukawa, rata and flax. In autumn they feed on small fruits and invertebrates. In winter months male birds frequently fly from offshore islands to mainland Northland to feed in suburban gardens, but females do not migrate. Bellbirds raise two broods a year, building a nest of twigs, leaves and grasses in a thick shrub or fork of a tree. On some offshore islands, such as Hen Island, bellbirds build their nest in shallow cavities of trees. This is probably as a protection against damage by petrels flying in at night to their nests. Females incubate the clutch of three or four eggs for 14 days, and chicks, which are fed by both parents, fledge when three weeks old. Recent reports have indicated that some bellbirds are breeding on the Whangaparaoa Peninsula. These birds have probably flown from the nearby Tiritiri Matangi Island sanctuary, where bellbirds are numerous.

125

MELIPHAGIDAE

Tui are the largest and best known of the honeyeaters. They are widely distributed throughout New Zealand and offshore islands. Although primarily a forest bird, tui are also common in suburban gardens where they will readily take sugar water from bird tables. Tui tend to migrate to other areas to take nectar, when trees such as kowhai and pohutukawa are flowering. The birds are important in dispersing the seeds of most species of podocarp trees and in pollinating many flowering plants such as flax, mistletoe, puriri and kohekohe. Tui also feed on insects and spiders, sometimes taking moths on the wing. They will eat large insects, such as stick insects, cicadas and wasps. Male tui are aggressive when feeding on certain nectar-bearing trees, chasing away bellbirds and even female tui. The birds nest from September to January. The female builds a very bulky nest composed of sticks and grasses, lined with fine grasses and a few feathers. The nest is placed in a tree fork or in dense shrub. In many mainland areas where rats are common, nests are often built high in the canopy of kanuka trees. The usual clutch consists of two or three pink, brown-spotted eggs incubated by the female for 14 days. The chicks are fed by both parents with nectar, small fruits and insects. Chicks fledge when three weeks old.

### Yellowhammer *Emberiza citrinella* 16 cm

Yellowhammers were introduced to New Zealand from Europe in the 1860s. They are now very common throughout the country, favouring open country where there are hedgerows, or rough pastures with gorse and brambles. In autumn and winter, yellowhammers form flocks, sometimes mingling with greenfinches and goldfinches. Their diet consists of seeds from grasses and shrubs as well as invertebrates, including earthworms. They also feed on ripe fruits, especially blackberries. Nests are built close to the ground, in rough herbage on banks and under brambles or gorse. The nest is composed of grasses and lichens and lined with horsehair or sometimes wool. Two broods are raised between September and February. The clutch of three or four eggs is incubated by the female, with the male taking short spells at incubating. Chicks hatch in 14 days and fledge in another 14 days.

### Cirl bunting *Emberiza cirlus* 16 cm

A small number of cirl buntings were introduced to New Zealand from Britain in the 1870s. They are now found mainly in the drier regions of Marlborough and Otago in the South Island, with small numbers scattered from Northland to Gisborne in the North Island. They are now extremely rare in England, their country of origin. Male cirl buntings and yellowhammers are easily distinguished, but the females and immature birds of both these species are somewhat similar. The yellowhammer can be recognised by its russet-coloured lower back. Cirl buntings inhabit open country with hedges, brambles and matagouri bushes. They feed on seeds from grasses and other vegetation, but take invertebrates when nesting. The nest of dry grasses and lichen is built in dense shrubbery or clumps of brambles. The female incubates the clutch of three or four eggs for 12 days and chicks fledge when 12 days old.

127

**Chaffinch** *Fringilla coelebs* 15 cm

*Chaffinch: male (top); female (bottom).*

Of the four species of finches introduced to New Zealand in the 1860s, the chaffinch is probably the most familiar, as it frequently visits urban gardens. In flight, chaffinches can be distinguished from other finches by their broad white shoulder patch and prominent white outer tail feathers. They inhabit open farmlands, orchards and gardens and are the only introduced finch to be found in the depths of native forests. They may also be seen in alpine herbfields and are found on many offshore islands. Chaffinches feed on seeds and fruits of many plants, including native shrubs and trees. However, as finches have powerful beaks, they crush the seed and so do not assist in dispersal. Apart from their main diet of seeds, chaffinches take a wide range of invertebrates, particularly caterpillars. Like other finches, chaffinches form flocks during autumn and winter, feeding on seeds in pastures and orchards. In the South Island large flocks often feed on fallen grain in cereal stubble fields, sometimes accompanied by greenfinches. However, in suburban areas, birds frequently remain as single pairs. Chaffinches rear two broods a year, from September to January, in a neat, compact nest of grasses, moss and sometimes wool. The outside is a covering of lichens bound with spiderweb. The female incubates the clutch of three or four turquoise, brown-streaked and spotted eggs for 13 days, the chicks then being fed by both parents before fledging in 14 days.

## Goldfinch *Carduelis carduelis* 13 cm

Goldfinches were introduced to New Zealand from Britain in the 1860s and are now more common here than in their country of origin. They are seen throughout the country and offshore islands, in rough pastures, orchards, country roadsides and suburban parks. They are easily identified by their small size and colourful plumage. Sexes are similar in colour. Apart from feeding on seeds of grasses and various weeds, goldfinches eat small insects, such as aphids as well as spiders. During winter months they form very large flocks, feeding on grass seeds and particularly thistle heads. At these times they are often joined by other finches. Nesting takes place from October to February. The birds construct a very neat nest of dry grasses, lichen, moss and sometimes wool. The favourite site is in an orchard tree as well as gorse or shrubs. The four or five pale blue, brown-streaked and spotted eggs are incubated by the female for 12 days. The chicks fledge when 14 days old.

## Greenfinch *Carduelis chloris* 15 cm

The greenfinch, introduced from Britain in the 1860s, is very common throughout most areas of New Zealand. They inhabit farmland, rough pastures, scrubland and sand dunes, where there is a covering of vegetation. Greenfinches feed on a variety of seeds and take maize and other cereals from stubble, their strong beaks being able to crush large seeds. They also feed on vegetation and invertebrates. The birds are double brooded, nesting from October to February. The large nest, built in hedges, gorse, matagouri or pines, is composed of grasses, lichens and small twigs, and lined with fine grasses. Four or five pale green, darkly brown-marked eggs are incubated by the female for 14 days. She is fed at the nest by the male, and he also helps feed the chicks. Like other finches, food is regurgitated from the crop. Chicks fledge at 15 days old.

The redpoll is the smallest of the finches that were introduced from Britain in the 1860s. They are now very common throughout the country and some offshore islands. The birds inhabit rough pastures, scrublands, coastal sand dunes, tussock lands and alpine herbfields at high altitudes. They are most common in the drier regions of the South Island. Like other finches, redpolls feed on seeds of grasses and weeds, except when nesting. Generally their intake of invertebrate food is limited. Nesting extends from August to February. The nest and eggs are similar to those of the goldfinch, but it is not as tidy and more grasses are used. Nests are built in gorse, brambles, hedges and orchard fruit trees. The female incubates for 11 days and chicks fledge when 14 days old.

# House sparrow *Passer domesticus* 14 cm

*House sparrows, male on left.*

The ubiquitous house sparrow was introduced to New Zealand in the 1860s, and as the birds rear three or four broods a year, they quickly colonised the whole country. The birds inhabit farmlands, orchards and urban environments. After nesting they form large flocks, roosting in city trees and tall hedgerows. Sparrows eat a variety of seeds and fruits and take invertebrates when feeding chicks. They cause considerable damage to ripening corn crops, especially in the South Island. House sparrows nest from September to January, building a domed nest of grasses with an entrance hole on one side. The clutch of three or four variable-coloured eggs is incubated by both sexes for 12 days, and chicks fledge when 15 days old.

## Starling *Sturnus vulgaris* 21 cm

Starlings, introduced to New Zealand in the 1860s, are now very common throughout the country, inhabiting farmlands, orchards, forest fringes and parks and gardens. They feed on a variety of invertebrates, and are beneficial to agriculture as they probe to eat harmful grass grubs, although they also cause damage to orchard fruits.

Starlings often feed in flocks on fruiting podocarp trees, especially kahikatea. The birds also sip nectar from flax flowers, resulting in a red pollen-covered head. Starlings nest in tree holes, buildings and crevices in cliffs. They readily accept garden nest boxes, which the male starling visits through many months of the year. Their nesting season is restricted, with most eggs being laid in October. A large quantity of nesting material is used, mainly of sticks and grasses. Both sexes share incubation of the four or five pale blue eggs for 12 days, and chicks fledge when 20 days old.

## Myna *Acridotheres tristis* 24 cm

Mynas were first introduced to the South Island in the 1870s. Preferring a warmer climate, they gradually spread to the North Island, and are now very common in Northland. Mynas inhabit agricultural land, orchards and suburban gardens, and are seen on roadsides where they take insects killed by traffic. The birds feed on a range of invertebrates and fruits of native and exotic trees. Mynas build nests in tree holes, clay banks and starling nest boxes. They often raise two broods in a season, the first in November. As they nest in holes, they have sometimes evicted native kingfisher from their nests. Both myna sexes incubate the three or four blue eggs for 14 days and chicks fledge when nearly four weeks old.

The endemic kokako is a threatened species, surviving only in mature, unmodified mixed podocarp forests in the North Island, and on some predator-free offshore islands where the birds have been relocated. A few populations exist in some Northland kauri forests. It has been proved that competition for food, predation of eggs, chicks and incubating birds by brush-tailed possums is responsible for the declining kokako populations. However, remarkable results of successful breeding have resulted in areas where extensive predator control has been applied. Kokako sing in a hauntingly melodious tone, usually only heard soon after dawn. The birds are weak fliers, and seem to bound through the forest, using their long legs. They fly only short distances. They feed on a wide variety of succulent foliage, flowers and fruits and more particularly when feeding chicks, they take insects and spiders. When food is plentiful, especially in areas managed by intensive predator control, kokako raise two broods of chicks each year. The usual nesting season extends from November to March. The female builds a large nest with a base of sticks overlaid with small ferns, lichen and moss. Two or three cream, brown-spotted eggs are incubated by the female for 20 days. At some nests, males have been reported as sharing incubation. Both parents feed the chicks with fruit, vegetable pulp and insects. Chicks fledge when four and a half weeks old, accompanying and fed by the parents for several weeks.

**Saddleback** *Philesturnus carunculatus* 25 cm

*Saddleback: male (top); female (bottom).*

Saddlebacks disappeared from mainland New Zealand, due to predation by rats, cats and mustelids. In 1964 the only population of the North Island saddleback survived on Hen Island off the coast of Northland. A small number of the South Island subspecies inhabited islands off the Stewart Island south coast. Since 1965 several birds from both these species have been successfully transferred to other predator-free islands. The North Island saddleback is now well established and off the endangered list. However, due to their frequent habit of feeding on the ground, as they search for insects in the forest floor litter, the presence of predators will prevent their establishment on mainland New Zealand. Saddlebacks feed on a variety of insects and their larvae, spiders and fruit. They also take nectar from flax flowers and other plants. They delve into the bark of trees searching out insects, often accompanied by fantails which catch the disturbed flying insects. Saddlebacks hold large insects and case moth larvae in one foot, parrot-fashion, while they eat the succulent morsels. The birds rear three broods a season, in a nest of twigs and bark pieces, lined with fine grasses and built in a tree hole or cavity. The usual clutch consists of two to four eggs, incubated by the female for 18 days. The male calls her from the nest to feed her every 50 minutes. Both parents feed the chicks, which fledge when three weeks old.

## Australian magpie *Gymnorhina tibicen* 41 cm

White-backed and black-backed magpies were introduced to New Zealand in the 1860s. They have interbred, so that pied forms exist, with variations in the black plumage of the birds' backs. Magpies are now common in hill-country pastures, arable land and in many sheltered coastal areas. Magpies feed on a wide variety of invertebrates, vegetation and seeds. They rob eggs and young from other birds, particularly the ground nesters, such as pipits and skylarks. In some regions where these birds were common, the arrival of magpies in the locality completely eliminated the birds within three years. Magpies nest from May to November. They build a nest of sticks, lined with grasses and sheep wool in pine or macrocarpa trees, in crowns of treeferns and in coastal pohutukawa trees. The three or four greenish, brown-marked eggs are incubated by the female for three weeks. Both parents feed the chicks, which fledge when four weeks old.

**Rook** *Corvus frugilegus* 45 cm

Rooks were introduced to New Zealand in the 1860s. They have been slow in expanding their territories. The birds are beneficial to agriculture as they eat grass grubs. However, they have been declared a pest, particularly in Hawke's Bay, where they cause considerable damage to various crops. They are now confined to parts of Hawke's Bay, Canterbury and near Miranda on the Firth of Thames. Their diet consists of invertebrates, particularly grass grubs, earthworms and insects. They eat a variety of vegetation, including the growing crops of peas and cereals as well as acorns. Rooks nest in small colonies in trees such as pines and oaks. The nest is a bulky structure composed of sticks and leaves, lined with grasses. Three or four greenish, brown-marked eggs are laid in August or September and incubated by the female for 18 days. Chicks fledge when five weeks old.

# Further reading

*Checklist of the Birds of New Zealand*. E.G. Turbott, Ornithological Society of New Zealand Inc. Random Century, 1990.

*Field Guide to the Birds of New Zealand*. Ornithological Society of New Zealand. Viking, 1996.

*Field Guide to New Zealand Seabirds*. Brian Parkinson. New Holland Publishers (NZ) Ltd, 2000.

*New Zealand's Unique Birds*. Brian Gill, Geoff Moon. Reed Publishing (NZ) Ltd, 1999.

*Reed Field Guide to New Zealand Birds*. Geoff Moon. Reed Publishing (NZ) Ltd, 1992, and Reprints.

*Seabirds*. Peter Harrison. Croom Helm Ltd, 1986.

*Shorebirds*. P. Hayman, J. Marchant, T. Prater. Croom Helm Ltd, 1986.

*Shorebirds of Australia*. J.D. Pringle. Angus & Robertson Publishers, 1987.

*Wader Studies in New Zealand*. Ornithological Society of New Zealand, 1999.

# Index

# Notes

# Notes

# Notes

# Other titles in New Holland's Photographic Guide series:

**Seashells**
*Margaret S. Morley*
*Photographs by*
*Iain A. Anderson*
978 1 86966 044 7

**Sea Fishes**
*Wade Doak*
978 1 87724 695 1

**Mammals**
*Carolyn M. King*
*Photographs by*
*Rod Morris*
978 1 86966 202 8

**Trees**
*Lawrie Metcalf*
978 1 87724 657 9

**Wildflowers**
*Geoff and Liz Brunsden*
978 1 86966 047 5

**Alpine Plants**
*Lawrie Metcalf*
978 1 86966 128 1

**Ferns**
*Lawrie Metcalf*
978 1 87724 694 4

**Mushrooms and Fungi**
*Geoff Ridley*
*Photographs by*
*Don Horne*
978 1 86966 134 2

**Rocks & Minerals**
*Nick Mortimer,*
*Hamish Campbell*
*and Margaret Low*
978 1 86966 283 7

**Insects**
*Brian Parkinson*
*Photographs by*
*Don Horne*
978 1 86966 151 9

**Reptiles & Amphibians**
*Tony Jewell*
*Photographs by*
*Rod Morris*
978 1 86966 203 5